OCEANS APART

A MURDER MYSTERY

JEROME RABOW, PH.D.

ISBN 978-1-950818-94-5 (paperback)

Copyright © 2020 by Jerome Rabow, Ph.D.

All rights reserved. No part of this publication may be reproduced, distributed, or transmitted in any form or by any means, including photocopying, recording, or other electronic or mechanical methods without the prior written permission of the publisher. For permission requests, solicit the publisher via the address below.

Rushmore Press LLC
1 800 460 9188
www.rushmorepress.com

Printed in the United States of America

CHAPTER 1

The silence was broken by the slaps of gentle, tiny waves and an eight-year-old exulting over his skipping rocks three times before they disappeared in the incoming wave. A young girl shivered as she prepared to plunge in with her lithe body, hair up swept, without a cap. She dove, came up screaming as she ran to a beach chair to a man waiting with a large towel that he wrapped slowly and tightly around her. And there is silence again. Detective Joe Zuma relished the quiet that he knew would end when he returned to work at the 25th precinct in Santa Monica .He knew this time when he could turn off his mind was precious. He did not have to watch everything… how people communicate, the clothing they wore, the watches or rings on their hands, the cars they drive or the magazines they read. He is off duty and there is only the movement of the waves and the few figures on the beach.

    The gulls were screeching. The wind had picked up, was turning cooler, and people were beginning to pick up their umbrellas and beach towels and head to the parking lot. Joe also decided to leave his bench sitting view of the shoreline and walk to the house he had been renting for his week off from work. A 40-ish female who had been sitting on the bench next to him got up, smiled and began walking towards her car. He was pleased to see her smile knowing that at 62,women were still checking him out. He did notice the car and her bag and bikini. She was not likely to be a suspect. Too bad, he thought, that this is cape cod instead of the bluffs in the Pacific Palisades. He decided to just wave back and not initiate any conversation. The ocean was completely empty now and the only sounds after the cars left were the lapping of waves and the gulls. Two fishermen had come to the edge of the bay either to get the stripper bass that were soon going to be out of season or perhaps, and Joe didn't know this, might be on their way passing through the Cape Cod Bay into the Atlantic.

"Oh my god that was a really bad idea "were the last words he heard from the seashore as a young boy took his plunge trying to follow the path of the stones he had been skipping.

Joe smiled and waved at the passing car with the woman who had gazed at him earlier. Too bad, he thought as he saw her looking in her rear view mirror. Joe thought she might be hoping for a stop sign from him in case he might change his mind. "No Darling, I wish I could but I'm leaving tomorrow." he thought.

CHAPTER 2

Phil Lyons stepped out on the balcony at Shutters Hotel in Santa Monica. He wanted to smell the salt air despite the oppressive heat. The sun was setting as he watched the six surfers who would keep going until it would no longer feel safe in the dark. This was his favorite rendezvous place for him and his lover. They had tried many spots along the California coast but the view from this, the highest floor felt the safest. It was distant from each of their homes and the height made him feel that he was removed from the turmoil of his life. He had planned to have their dinner brought to the room about half an hour before sunset so they could drink champagne, toast each other and watch the ocean and sky change colors. When she arrived she greeted him with a strong embrace. He imagined she wanted to make love immediately. He asked her to wait till after dinner, which would be arriving momentarily.

"Sure, darling. I'll unpack while we're waiting and change into something lighter so we can sit on the balcony."

Phil was unsure whether he should talk to her while they were having their drink or wait until after dinner when they would both be a bit tipsy. She was expecting him to have made a decision as to when he was going to leave his marriage. His sales had dipped at the Porsche dealership in the last few months and he believed he needed a few more months before he could afford to leave and would tell his wife that he was leaving. After dinner he told her about the financial hardships that had developed.

"Well Phil, how much do you feel you need so you could leave?"

"It's not just the amount of money, it's knowing that customers are coming back and that Porsche it's a luxury car that folks are willing to pay for. It's not a Ford that people need.

"That could be indeterminate: I don't want any more waiting in my life."

"Car sales always turn around, darling, please be patient."

"Please tell me how much you need. I can give you $15,000 right away."

"I don't feel comfortable taking money from you."

She raised her voice. "Well I don't feel comfortable waiting and waiting. You have already had two postponements."

"Alright, let me sleep on it. I will let you know in the morning."

To herself, Madeline thought, "Sorry pal, you will not get that chance." She was glad she had prepared for this.

CHAPTER 3

This was his last day of his annual rent for a house in Truro, the last day for visiting families who could be there. He had done it for over 12 years with Carol and he did not want to stop after she was killed in a driving accident.

Tomorrow he will be on a plane back to Los Angeles. His older boys would also be leaving but on separate flights to Northern California. The reunions were always sparked by the energy of the younger people while Joe and the other elders discussed illnesses, passing and politics.

His last night in Truro was spent with his two sons. Josh and David, in Wellfleet, which offered more options and better restaurants than Truro. It was something that the three of them had been doing on the last day of their vacation. The older boy, Josh, drove, as Joe knew he would be drinking on this bon voyage dinner. They managed to get a parking spot right in front of the Winslow Tavern; after rejecting a table on the patio, they went inside and ordered drinks.

The boys began talking. Josh was gleeful about how he had learned to paddle board and how far he had been able to go out in the bay and to even paddle half way towards Provincetown from Truro. David, who was an excellent swimmer for his college team at The University of California, Davis and did triathlons in the off season, said how wonderfully different it was to swim in salt water and how he could swim out over two miles from shore when the tide was low and the people on the beach looked like they tiny insects.

"The patrol boats had me go in dad as they said sharks had been spotted off Provincetown. When I get back to school l can tell my teammates that I was swimming with the sharks."

Joe reminded Josh that he could continue to work on Paddle Boarding at UC Davis and asked David for the date of his next triathlon . When the drinks came, Joe raised his glass "To us, to our coming back next year and to Carol… After a pause Joe picked up the menu and said

"Lets order."

Joe knew what the three of them would order. After a week of fish, mussels and clams they would all go for the best steak in the house.

He looked at his boys, thought of Carol, and what fine young men they were turning out to be and how she might have felt about them.

"Dad, what's the matter?

Oh I was thinking of your Mom… Josh interrupted; "Yeah, I could always tell when you get that far away look that it must be about Mom. But don't start to tell us how proud she would be. Instead of that, let's talk about how totally nuts you were when Mom got killed. I wasn't sure if you would make it."

"Yeah Dad. It's lucky we had each other. Josh and I would talk every night about how absent, and gloomy and angry you were. We had bets on how late you would turn up from looking for the drunk driver. I won money because no matter what David said I always said it would be later."

"Yeah Dad, I had to pay him 10 bucks. How about reimbursing me? I will take cash or a check.

Joe laughed and pulled out a ten-dollar bill. "I'm really sorry. I never realized how hard it must have been for you. I was wrapped up in my own grief, and the booze wasn't helping me be aware of the two of you and your needs. I think it was my rage that blinded me. I guess I forgot that you were hurting also. I hope that is now in the past and that you are no longer hurting."

Josh spoke. "I'm o.k. Dad. Nothing to worry about. Mostly I'm glad that you're back and back fully."

"Amen to that", said David "And now we can just dig in to a very un-PC meal. Good old red meat. If I see another fish I might throw it at Josh. Let us carnivores do our thing."

When the diners arrived Joe dropped his head. He was glad that his boys could not see the tears in the corner of his eyes. They had seen him cry before. He had done a lot of it after Carol was killed, but he thought this might spoil their farewell evening.

"After we finish I propose we get desert just around the corner. No need to drive. It's the Bliss Shop for Heavenly Ice Cream."

As they stepped out of the restaurant and walked towards the sidewalk, past the diners on the patio, Joe spotted the woman he had seen earlier in the day.

She was sitting alone, and drawing while she sipped her wine.

"Hi. I'm sorry to interrupt you, I didn't say hello earlier but would like to say 'hi' now."

"Hi."

"May I see your drawing?"

"Actually you can have it. I was finishing it up."

Joe looked at what she had drawn. It was the edges of the Wellfleet housetops against the evening sky. She had managed to show the outline of the Wellfleet homes by penciling in a very, dark, almost black, greyish sky.

"I like it. It's very much how I see it. You have captured it."

She signed and handed it to him.

"It's yours."

Joe took it but could not understand her handwriting except to see that her first name began with a C. He could also see that she had written down her phone number.

CHAPTER 4

She had not signed into the hotel. Nor had she used the valet parking. Rather, she had parked in a 24-hour lot with her credit card and despite the heat walked the three blocks to the hotel. She had carried only a small bag so as not to draw attention and have a bellhop offer to help. She walked through the lobby not looking at anyone so that everyone would imagine that she was a registered guest and walked into the ladies bathroom to cool off. She did not want Phil to wonder why she had walked instead of parking in the hotel. She went straight up to his room believing that she would be unnoticed and as invisible as possible.

She wasn't that surprised when he told her that he wasn't ready to leave his wife. She was prepared for his desire for another extension. She also knew that he would not take the money she had offered him. Not that he would have the chance to say yes. After dinner she brought out the coke and Phil was surprised

"Well I thought we would be celebrating your breakup, But since we can't celebrate that lets just enjoy ourselves. She laid out four lines of coke and they each snorted two lines.

"You think of everything Madeline. There's no one who can plan better than you. I think of you whenever I hear that song, "You are the wind beneath my wings.'

She smiled to herself and thought, 'I have to. I have two lovers and a husband who is as unreliable as they come. I have had to learn the hard way to take charge of everything and to plan for all possibilities.'

"That's one of the reasons you have me in your life. I brought the money just in case and I brought the coke just in case."

Their lovemaking was passionate but short with Phil falling asleep immediately. Madeline realized that this would be the last time. She had enjoyed it and enjoyed the secrecy of it all 'I will say good-bye to you but you will not be able to do the same.' She reached into her small purse and took out the needle and slowly injected into his thigh. He twitched slightly but did not wake. It took about ten minutes before Phil Lyons left this world.

She methodically went through the room washing her prints off the glasses and silverware and put the tray outside the door. She saw his phone and went through her plan to leave it there. The lobby of the hotel was almost empty and with her head down she would have looked like a gal who had paid a visit to a male guest but there was no one who noticed. The parking lot was also empty. She wrapped the needle in a plastic bag and threw it into the blue, recycling trash can, which she knew would grind it up with any other metals. The only evidence of another person's presence was the dinner that was ordered for two. That was not evidence against her but would probably further serve to have investigators believe that Phil Lyons was having too many difficulties and took his own life after having sex with a call girl. Even if they were suspicious of foul play because there were no fingerprints on the glasses or dishes she felt she was in the clear.

The ride home took a half an hour and her husband was already sleeping. She fell asleep believing that she had simplified her life. She would probably get a call from the police after they found the phone. This is what she wanted. There will be no more wind beneath your wings, my friend. Phil's words played in her head as she nodded off. "You think of everything Madeline."

CHAPTER 5

While licking their ice cream sugar cones, David asked. "What did that lady say to you Dad?"

"She didn't say much but she gave me her drawing."

"How come? Just out of the blue?"

"Well she also wrote her phone no on it."

"Way to go pops. Yes, You are back."

On the drive back to their rental, Joe dialed the number.

"Hello, you've reached the studio of Claudia Berlin. If you would like to make an appointment, leave me your telephone number and a time you could visit."

"Hi Claudia, I would like to make an appointment. But since I wont be able to visit for nine months, I think I had better call you back in June. I live in L.A. and visit yearly. Oh and this is the proud recipient of your Wellfleet drawing, Joe Zuma."

The two boys exchanged looks, smiled and nodded to each other as if to say, way to go dad.

They had to get ready for an early departure so they emptied the dishwasher, threw out all the food that they had not used, swept the floors, took out the garbage and went to bed. They had perfected this routine. They had to get up early to make sure everything in the rental house was clean and ready for the next renters. They also had to drop off the keys to the rental house at the Duarte rental agency in Truro, return all the linens to The Furies in Wellfleet, and do the 2 1/2 hour drive to Boston's Logan Airport.

Both boys slept on the drive and Joe drove straight through to Logan airport waking them up just as they were ready to be dropped off to their different terminals. Josh would be landing in Reno and David would be flying to San Jose.

Their goodbyes, with sleepy eyes and quick pecks was a bit wrenching to Joe as he was not sure when exactly he would see them again but also knowing that next year at the cape they would be older and possibly at the point where they might not even want to or be able to take their vacation at the same time Joe took his. Joe went to drop off the rental, and would be flying directly to Los Angeles. landing at 9.p.m. His assistant Patrick Cruz called while Joe was getting on the plane and offered to pick him up.

"Pat it's crucial that we separate official business from personal affairs. We cannot do anything that is personal and costs the taxpayers money. I know you mean well but we always have to do the right thing. We can never even stop to drop off our laundry while on duty. Pick up your damn donuts before you are assigned to be at work. Buy enough of them so you don't have to stop in on company time to get more. This is important. If your going to continue to work for me and do the excellent work you are already doing you must always separate your personal stuff from the professional."

"Ok boss, I got it. No problem. I'll see you in the morning when you get in."

Joe liked Pat Cruz a lot. He was the sharpest of all the new appointments that Joe had mentored over the years. He had wanted to enlist in order to serve but his mom had convinced him he could serve without going so far away that she would only see him occasionally. He finished the Police Academy with the highest grades and Joe was very happy to have someone so young who was eager to learn and whom he could rely on. The Cruz family had invited Joe for Christmas and he saw what a hard working family they were. It made him feel at home as he remembered how his grandparents, who had also emigrated to America, enjoyed Christmas and their better life in America and who knew they could have, through hard work, a better life for their children, which meant Joe's father.

CHAPTER 6

"Welcome back boss." The greeting from Pat was as sincere as his "I missed you. How was your trip? And holiday? I hope it went well with you and your boys."

"Thanks, Pat, it was really special this time. They are growing up and asking questions and now can even make fun of me. They told me what a disaster I was after Carol was killed. I have no doubt that you would agree with them."

"It was pretty bad boss but we survived and the toll was on you. I knew I had to keep a close eye on our cases and I don't think any of them were messed up."

"Thanks Pat, Tell me what I missed and bring me up to date."

"You didn't miss much but we do have a murder. Came in early this morning. White male found dead in one of our cities' loveliest hotels. A Mr. Phil Lyons. Looks like suicide. Wallet still intact, cash and cards there."

"What else do we know?"

"We know his name and residence. He checked in alone but had a visitor. The hotel confirmed there was a dinner order for two that came in around 5. Delivered at

6:30. The bellhop who delivered it saw a woman's clothing on the couch. We searched the room for prints but found none. There were some traces of coke and the ME said that the guy had injected a massive amount of coke. The dinner plates had already been run through the dishwasher."

"What do you think Pat?

"I think it's weird that there are no prints. If it's a hooker and the guy died, a hooker would take the cash but would not worry too much about getting rid of all the prints in the room and the plates or dishes. Looks like a professional job to me.

It could be a suicide. The guy or gal didn't want anyone to know about the hooker, or trace her. They were pretty careful about prints."

"You may be right, boss. He looks pretty young and healthy for a suicide."

"O.K. Pat, call the residence and see if anyone lives there."

"Done boss. There's a wife."

"Oh, Oh. Shit I guess we are going to deliver the bad news. Did you tell her anything?"

"No Boss, I just said we were interested in speaking with her husband and asked if he was at home. She said he wasn't and hadn't come home since yesterday morning. She asked what this was about and I just told her it was routine ."

"Call her Pat and set up an appointment. Come with me. I want you there to see how she takes it."

"Sure Boss, let me grab my donut."

The crumbs from his Dunkin Donuts always spilled over the side of his coffee cup. Zuma knew that habit would end if and when Pat would marry. At this point Zuma thought he was T.U. Terminally Uncommitted. He didn't worry about his finding someone .Pat was good looking, smart and had always expressed a wish to have kids. Zuma had seen him around children in his cases and he was always good with them.

.

O.K thought Zuma. 'The week is not starting with a dramatic murder but with what looks like a simple murder or it might be a suicide. . Zuma corrected himself knowing that there had never been a murder that he worked on that was a simple murder. He knew that this would be the beginning of complexity.

CHAPTER 7

A woman answered the door. It was five in the afternoon but the woman was still in her bathrobe.

"Good Afternoon, Mrs. Lyons. We're here to ask you a few questions about your husband. We're from the Santa Monica Police Department. I'm afraid we have some bad news for you. Your husbands' body was found in a Santa Monica hotel last night."

Zuma watched carefully registering the woman's grief. She seemed genuinely shocked but not surprised.

"Damn it. I told him that sales would be coming back to normal. They always do. The car business is always going up and down. I pleaded with him to be patient."

"So your husband sold cars in the local Porsche dealership. Did you notice anything unusual in the past few months about him that you can describe?"

"I know he wasn't sleeping very well. I would hear him get up two or three times a night. When I asked him if anything was bothering him he said no but he also seemed defensive. Of course I worried."

"What did you worry about?"

"That he would take his own life."

"So you think it was a suicide."

"I don't know. You said his body was found in a hotel so if you knew more I assume you would have said he was murdered.

"At this point we're not ruling anything out. Can you please tell us what he was unhappy about?"

"The business. It is and it always was the business. He was the top salesperson at his company and sales had fallen off. The entire industry was in a slump. I told him to have faith. That this was not his fault. This was what life handed you and you just had to accept."

"Was there anything else Mrs. Lyons that you felt was unusual in the past few months?"

"He seemed to be making a lot more phone calls, I thought that this was part of his efforts to sell more."

"And when did those phone calls start?"

"I think it was a bit more than a year ago."

"Was there anything else?"

"No, not that I can think of."

"Sorry to ask you at this time but how did you and your husband get along?

"Oh, Detective we were a normal couple .I had been unhappy in the beginning with his inattentiveness and forgetting and his constant focus on the business. We don't have kids so there could have been a lot of things we could have done as a couple. But I came to accept it. I found my work as a RN very fulfilling. In recent years I have had to accept more as he seemed to be less interested in our marriage."

"Can you date when that diminished interest in your marriage began?"

"I would say it's been about a year and half."

"So that happened before the auto industry collapsed. What do you think may have been going on?"

"Detective Zuma, I'm a married woman and I would imagine it's hard for any married woman in America to believe that her husband is going to be faithful after 10 years. I assumed if he was unfaithful that he would come back to me and I didn't want to put any energy into tracking him down or worrying about it. I accept this about men in general and my husband in particular."

"Did he have friends outside of work?

'I was his friend. I don't think there was anyone else besides me who he would consider to be a friend. He is, I guess now I need to say, he was a pretty quiet guy when it came to talking about himself.

When there was something bothering him I learned that I would just have to wait. He worked at the dealership for 15 years so I had time to figure it out. And I did"

"Do you think he might have spoken to anyone there about what was going on?"

"I don't know. Maybe. He was much more gregarious at work. He was always friendly but probably never about personal matters."

"Can you provide us with a phone number where he worked so we could speak to some of his colleagues. The name of the manager that would also be helpful."

"Sure .I can do that. When will I be able to see the body?"

"We have to run a few tests but I will have Pat or myself call you as soon as we know anything. Thank you Mrs. Lyons as soon as we have some more information we will be speaking with you and we may have to come back for another visit. I do have one more question. How did you spend last night?"

"Oh my god do you believe that I could have had anything to do with his death? That is outrageous. Do I seem to you the kind of wife who would do that? I told you I was prepared for him to have an affair and end an affair and for us to live out our lives, whatever they would be like as a couple. Just like so many other couples do when there has been an affair.

"I'm sorry but it is routine that we verify the whereabouts of all persons connected to a victim.

"Well I went to my Alanon meeting, I think it was over at seven and came directly home. I usually go to bed by nine or nine thirty but since Phil hadn't come back I waited until past ll. Once I go to sleep I sleep through. I had to get up early

"Oh and remind us of what you do. I think you said you're an RN,

"Yes I am and I work at the hospital and as I said I had to be in for my early shift at seven. It's not my favorite since patients are groggy and cranky but I do have to take it once in a while even though I'm a senior nurse on the staff."

"I assume you do give injections and are able to measure dosages for all kinds of drugs."

"My God, detective you are so obvious. Yes, I could have injected Phil with some overdose of morphine or some other drug that would have killed him. . BUT as I said before I had no desire to be rid of him."

"We will have to check on your presence at the Alanon meeting and at the hospital but we don't have to do that right away. Can you prepare them so they can verify your presence .We understand they would not want to talk to us unless you gave your permission."

"I'll speak to them."

"Thank you again Mrs. Lyons. Here's my card. In case you think of anything else that is important please call us."

"OK Pat what do you think?"

"I think she's an Alanon junkie who's got that 'Accept crap down pat .She also didn't seem that surprised or shocked about it being a suicide. AND I thought it a bit strange that she said "see the body, instead of see my husband's corpse or body. Sounded a bit cold or at best distant."

"She's a nurse used to dealing with death. Maybe it's just an occupational disease. I'm sure boss sometimes we sound that way to our suspects".

"I agree with that. We will probably have to come back and see what else was going on in their marriage besides acceptance and we will have to speak to her Alanon buddies. Can you check with the hospital? Also the increase in phone calls started with the decrease in sales, but it may have also been related to something else."

"Like another woman Boss?"

"Yes Pat. Let's head over to the Porsche dealership. You call the manager and tell him we are coming."

CHAPTER 8

"Hi Mr. Marshall. We want to speak to some of the people who work with Phil Lyons.

"Is something wrong? He was due in at 12 and he is usually very good about calling in.

"I'm afraid you have lost one of your employees. . His body was discovered two nights ago.

"Oh shit. God Damn. I knew he was upset with sales but he has always been able to pull out of our slumps. I thought he would be able to do it again.

"We have to ask a few questions to you and the others he worked with. What kind of employee was he?

"He was really good with customers, especially if kids were tagging along. He was my top sales person. He got along well with the other sales staff. He was flexible about his own vacation plans, willing to help out the others who had to adjust their vacations around their children's school schedules. Phil didn't have kids so he seemed understanding of those who did.

"Did he ever go out and socialize with others in sales?"

"Yes and I heard he would often buy a round of drinks. They guys said he was never that talkative."

"Which of your salespeople do you think he was closest too?"

"That would be Joe Calgrove, sitting right over there in his office. Shall I call him over?"

"No, we can just walk over to him."

"Hi Mr. Calgrove. We're from the Santa Monica Police Department and were investigating the death of Phil Lyons."

"Shit. Shit. Shit. I knew that something was up. When did this happen? I should've said more."

"What do you think was up? Please tell us as much as you know."

"Phil was never an upper. But in the past year or so he seemed more moody and depressed and other times he seemed hopeful and optimistic .His ups and downs didn't always seem related to the job? In the past his moods were closely linked to his sales."

"Did he ever speak to you about another woman?"

"Officers I don't want to get him in trouble or and I don't wanna get his wife upset. She's probably already pretty upset. I guess I should give her a call,

even though I only met her a few times at our Christmas parties."

"You were saying…another woman…."

"Oh yes, There was one evening, we were all drinking and on the way out of the restaurant Phil mentioned he was seeing someone on the side who was married but that he was very hopeful that she would be leaving. He said he was no longer attracted to or in love with his wife. When he spoke about the married woman he was quite happy. Happiness for Phil was not exactly his major suit."

"Did he mention her name to you?"

"Yes I don't remember it exactly because he only said it once . It was a French name, at least a French sounding name. I asked him a month or so later on what was going on and he said 'I'm still hoping and planning."

"Mr. Calgrove, do you think Phil Lyons talked to anyone else here that he worked with?"

"I'm pretty sure he didn't. He told me that I was the only one he felt he could share anything personal."

"Thank you for your help. We may want to check back with you if we have to. If you think of the name, please give us a call."

CHAPTER 9

"Boss the tech guys have gone through the Lyons's phone. There was one number that kept coming up quite regularly. We tracked it down. It belongs to Mrs. Madeline Couture. She lives close by in Culver City."

"Was there a call to her on the evening Lyons was killed?'

"Let's see, boss. Yes, the last call he made to her was at 5:30 P.M. He didn't make any calls after that."

"I'm going to call her now Pat. I'll put you on speaker."

Madeline saw the number that she had been expecting. She debated whether to pick it up and respond. She had hoped to be alone when the police called. She thought that this was even better than she had planned.

"Hi, Madeline Labelle speaking."

"Ms. Labelle, this is Detective Jo Zuma from the Santa Monica Police Department. I wonder if we can make an appointment to speak with you."

"Right now Detective I'm in a car. I'm driving to Arizona. I will be here for a few days. I'm working on a book about my father. He was an American military hero."

"When are you planning to come back?"

"Just a moment Detective let me ask my writing partner." Madeline made sure that Zuma would hear her question. "Larry how much time will we need?"

"Well I booked two nights in Phoenix and one night in Scottsdale."

"Detective, I guess I'll be back in three days. Can this wait?"

"It can. But in the interim I want to ask you if you knew a man by the name of Phil Lyons?"

"Yes I do. What do you mean knew? I know him very well."

"His body was found in a hotel."

"Oh man, I told him the slump in car sales would end soon. I guess he didn't believe me."

"So you were close to him?"

"Yes we were close, Detective. He and I were probably closer than he and his wife."

"Oh, How could that be?

"We were lovers for over a year."

Madeline signaled Larry to be quiet putting her finger over her mouth as he sat stunned with his mouth wide open.

"Mrs. Labelle, will you be able to account for your whereabouts last Friday night?"

"Sure detective. Shall I do that now or when we meet."

"Just tell me who could verify where you were."

"That would be my husband."

"O.K Let's plan to meet when you get back."

"What in hell's name did you mean when you told the dick that you had a lover?"

"I told him the truth Larry. I know you may not like to hear that but it gives us a better cover than before. No one will think that I'm doing anything with you besides writing a book. It's for us."

"Oh shit Madeline. How could you do that? How could you say that?"

"Larry stop whining. You now can have me all to yourself." She believed that that might reassure Larry even though she knew that it was not true. No man was ever going to have her all to himself. She had been captured by that dream early on in her marriage. Now her business and all the details of planning her life with a husband and one lover, instead of two, was what would capture her.

"Sure Detective. I'll call you when I get back into town."

"Tell me how long you had this Phil as your lover,

"Listen Larry. I don't have to tell you anything. You can decide if you want me to yourself and to continue to use our cover and have good times and make money the way we are doing or you can walk away from me and from the money making successful business that we have developed and run together."

"Shit, I don't care too much about the money. I can give it all to you if you promise me you won't take on another lover."

"I can promise you that. And I don't want to take a bigger percentage of our profits. I want to treat you fairly.

Fairly??? is not what you did with this Phil character. Fairly is your being honest with me. Fairly is not cheating on me."

I don't want to argue any more. You're right. I didn't treat you fairly but I can start right now. Let's check into the romantic hotel that you and I love so much. I would like to have a more than fair night of lovemaking with you."

Larry knew she was buying him off but he liked the price.

"And we don't have to spend all three nights away. We can get back early and do some business and then I will call that detective." Her plans had gone exactly as she had hoped. As they checked into The Phoenician, one of the classy hotels in Scottsdale, she recalled the old joke about 'if you want God to laugh tell him your plans.' She had told no one her plans. She was not laughing but a big smile was on her face.

CHAPTER 10

"Boss, this is one of those 'truth is stranger than fiction moments.' We just got a bulletin telling us that a woman's body was dumped near a trash can in Santa Monica. Two bullets from a Glock 38 were found in her chest. Her I D was still on her. This is the unbelievable part, boss. It was the woman you were just talking with three days ago, the one who said she would call when she got back from Arizona. Can you believe it boss? Madeline Couture said she was coming in and now she is dead. I guess we can eliminate her in the death of Phil Lyons."

"No Pat. Not necessarily. I'm not ready to accept that possibility. She still could be the killer. Someone else might have been jealous or angry at her because she was the lover."

"You're right boss, I guess we will have to go back to speak to the guy's wife."

"What else can you tell me about the Couture gal?"

"She lived in Huntington Beach, married to Gary Couture. He's self-employed and has a plumbing and tile business. I didn't call him. I didn't know what you would want to do first."

"I guess the week is beginning pretty dramatically. We get one corpse on Monday and another on Thursday. Let's drive out to Mr. Couture. I can call him from the car. Good time to get away as the phones will be ringing off the hook asking for comments about two murders in one week. The newspapers will be blasting headlines about our city becoming a haven for homicides."

CHAPTER 11

Hello Gary? This is Detective Zuma. I was calling about your wife, Madeline . Yes I understand you haven't heard from her. We need to speak with you.

You're at work now? Ok Can we meet on your lunch break? Good. Tell us where you want us to come. Ok McDonalds it shall be. Which one? I got it. Try and get a booth if you get there ahead of us. I will be bringing my associate with me.

The drive down the coast was pleasant, as the traffic had slowed after the early morning rush. The waves reminded him of his recent time at the cape and the difference it made to be at work and driving past waves in contrast to just sitting, watching and listening. He wondered if it was too soon to follow up with his message to Claudia Berlin.

Gary was ruddy and very broad shouldered. He had extraordinarily large biceps and strong looking fingers. Zuma noticed that Gary did not look directly at him and thought he detected suspicion and fear in Gary's eyes. Zuma was surprised at his sunburn but Gary explained that he was often outside on jobs because he worked with only one other employee as they pulled wheelbarrows with cement to finish bathrooms and kitchens. Zuma knew that installing tiles and cement with only one other employee was hard work.

"Mr. LaBelle I'm sorry to inform you that your wife's body was found last night in Santa Monica. We believe that there was foul play."

Gary LaBelle sat stone-faced. Zuma could not detect any emotion in his face. He sat there with a matter of fact attitude, as if he had just heard that the weather was going to be a repeat of the last day. His voice was also matter of fact, even with the questions

"What do you mean foul play? "I was worried that she hadn't come home. Do you mean she was murdered?"

"Yes, at this point we think so. I have to ask you a few questions."

"'I had nothing to do with any damn murder, and certainly not of my wife."

"Mr. LaBelle you may have had absolutely nothing to do with the murder but I still have to get a statement from you and to ask you a few questions."

. Zuma thought that Gary's voice sounded quite flat without much emotion but he thought it might be it due to shock. Or it might be to any anger and resentment he had towards his wife. The thought occurred to him that if Gary were guilty he would be trying to sound more emotional. But on the other hand it did not seem to Zuma that Gary was good at imagining what other people would like to hear in order for them to know what he might be feeling.

"Gary, My guess is that you're still in shock but if there's anything you can tell me about Madeline's life that might bear on this case? Did she have any close friends?

Were there people who disliked her?"

"Madeline had lots of people she would spend time on the phone with. I think there were two close girl friends. And she had one close male friend."

"If you can give me their names and phone numbers before I leave that would be great. Tell me about the male friend."

"His first name was Larry. I don't know his last name. Madeline said they were working on a book about her dead father. Her dad was quite the military hero. She was very proud of him and wanted to let the world know about him."

"Have you read any of her work?"

"I did in the beginning but I didn't like that she was being so personal about her growing up years and I criticized her for writing about that. So she stopped showing it to me. I thought there were details that her father would not want the world to know about."

"But he was dead. How would he know?"

"I know but just the same I thought, what's to be gained?"

Zuma thought that this man was not exactly reflective about life.

"Did you suspect, and I am sorry to ask you this but it might help, that there was an intimate relationship between your wife and Larry?

"I don't think so. She was religious and I believed she took her marriage vows seriously."

"And how did the two of you get along?" Zuma decided to be more direct. "How much fighting did you do?

"She was always on my case about my not charging enough in my business. She would also get pissed off at my drinking and eating at fast food places. I never saw much sense in picking up my clothes since I was planning on wearing them the next day. Hell I liked being able to just get out of bed and slip my pants on. That bugged the hell out of her. When I got fed up at hearing her bitching I did scream back. The police came a few times. Madeline never called them. I guess she didn't feel I was going to do anything to really hurt her. It must have been the neighbors who called."

"Did you ever hit her?"

Gary paused. It was his first pause and Zuma realized that he was calculating what this might mean to the detective.

"I did and she called the police. They hauled me in but she decided to not press charges."

"So you only hit her once?"

Gary paused again. Zuma knew this response would be critical."

"Yes that was the only time."

Zuma registered the first lie on the case.

"Now if you can write down the names and phone numbers of her girl friends and her writer collaborator that would be helpful."

"What do you mean collaborator?"

"The guy she was working on her book with."

He handed over a paper with names and numbers scrawled in a haphazard fashion. Larry's last name was missing.

"You didn't know the name of your wife's collaborator. That seems odd Mr. LaBelle.

They were spending a lot of time together."

"Why should I? She never called him anything but Larry. I never met the dude."

Zuma registered the quick-tempered defensiveness 'I'll bet her time spent writing also pissed you off.' Zuma thought. .

""Is there anyone else that you think I should know about?"

"Oh yea, Madeline was seeing a therapist. I went with her occasionally but I stopped. I thought there was too much personal stuff that the therapist wanted to know about. Madeline would mention my pants on the floor and our fights. That just seemed way too personal for me."

"You know his name of course?"

"Sure .His name was Jerry; Jerry Milgram. I have a card here somewhere. I thought I had better save it in case…"

"In case what Mr. LaBelle?"

"Oh I don't know, Detective. These last two years we just haven't spent much time and I was always a bit worried. Madeline was a very friendly gal and the world is an unfriendly place."

Zuma was surprised at Gary's ability to compare the world with his wife. Maybe he got that from one of his buddies.

"Thank you Mr. Couture. You have been very helpful. And again I'm very sorry for your loss. I may have to call upon you again."

'Why? I've told you everything I know."

Zuma registered this as the second lie.

"Yes, but as we discover more you may need to corroborate", Zuma realized that he'd better use a different word. "We may need to confirm or disconfirm facts.

Gary smiled and again Zuma saw the fear in Gary's eyes but this time there was also a bead of sweat that was at the tip of his ear lobe. On the drive back, Zuma asked Pat for his impressions.

"I did think he was frightened, boss, when you said you would probably be calling back. Also I didn't believe that he hit her only once. I'll check hospital records and that one police record he told us about as well as for other calls. That will be easy for us. The business with her collaborator sounded strange. How could he not know his name? And why would she want to work with someone so far away. Those would be good leads to follow up with."

Zuma smiled as Pat had uttered all the same thoughts and wonderings that he had recorded with his interview. It was comforting to see that Pat and he thought alike. I guess he is learning from me.

"Sure boss. This is quite a welcome back for you. Do you think there could be any connection between the two vics? It would seem impossible for there to be a connection. They lived pretty far from each other."

"Pat, I always told you that coincidences are rarely coincidences. I'm ready to be surprised if this is just a coincidence."

Pat was caught off guard by Joe's comment. How could Joe possibly think of the events as related. Maybe that's what having so much more experience does to cops. Everything is connected and to be examined

CHAPTER 12

"Dr. Milgram, this is detective Joe Zuma . I'm from the 25th precinct and I need some of your time. I think an hour would do it."

"What is this about?"

"It concerns your patient ... no, I should say your ex patent Madeline Couture .

"I'm happy to help detective Zuma but how did you get my name?"

"Her husband said that you had been working with her and that you might be able to give us some clues as to what was going on in her life. I have a warrant that will allow me to inspect your notes and your emails."

"I'm happy to help in whatever way I can. Can you come see me this afternoon between four and five? I have an opening"

Milgram was happy to set the appointment. This might turn out to be the 15th case of suicide or murder that Jerry Milgram would be involved with. That it was a detective who called made him feel that it must be a murder investigation. Who would want to murder Madeline? Why would he even assume it was Madeline.? The detective might be investigating a murder without it being Madeline.If it was Madeline,could it be her husband? That's the most immediate suspect when a wife is murdered. Maybe it was the writer she was working with?

For Milgram solving a murder mystery was very much like helping his patients solve their problems. With a murder there were lots of clues and leads that had to be followed up on and either eliminated or pursued. There were lots of back and forth aspects until it became clear as to whom the killer was and what needed to be done. With his clients it could also be a while before all the leads could be eliminated. It took time for all their positive and hopeful and naïve efforts or wishes had come to naught and until there was only one very clear direction for his client to pursue. Only then would clients' choices be explicit, clear and conscious. Leaving a mate or a job or staying. The costs of either one were now explored and the illusions about a partner or boss or job changing had been demolished. Jerry trusted that the client would make the decision that was in their best interest. Jerry was hopeful that he could be involved in eliminating some leads for Zuma and be helpful in whatever other ways he could.

CHAPTER 13

Detective Zuma had the kind of charm that Jerry knew was forced. The moment the detective smelled that he was close to the murderer the charm would be turned off and there would be a relentless pursuit and challenge of the details and narrative that the potential murderer had spun.

The charm continued." Dr. Milgram, I have a warrant to obtain all your emails and your notes but I also want to talk to you directly. Notes and emails do not capture all that you might sense about your patient so I appreciate your speaking with me directly and as honestly as possible"

"That's not a problem, Detective. As long as you have a warrant I am eager to help in any way. Can you tell me why you want to know about her? I noticed that you referred to her as my ex patient."

"She was murdered. Her body was found in Santa Monica, three nights ago."

"I think I knew that when you called me. It was pretty shocking but I sensed that is what you meant when you referred to her as my ex patient. And since you're a detective I figured you would want to talk about a murder. Let me tell you all I can about Madeline. I've known her for about four years. She was not a consistent client in this period of time. Sometimes she would not see me for two or three months. She had difficulty in her marriage with her husband's drinking, intermittent work and emotional outbursts that she often labeled as abuse. These things were very disturbing to her and she would often cancel appointments at the last minute.

"Is "abuse' your word or hers?"

"Her exact words were "Emotional and physical abuse." I have those words in my notes.

"Do you think he was capable of murdering his wife?"

"Detective Zuma, I'm sure we're both in a business where we have learned and know that people are capable of anything'"

Zuma smiled at that comment and moved back to his professional countenance.

"Her husband said that she had been spending a lot of time with a guy named Larry and they were involved in writing together. Do you know anything about their relationship?"

"If you're suggesting that it was romantic it could have been. She said that he helped give her some money when things were tight at home and even did some chores around the house that she was unable to do because of a bad back. The book she was working on had to do with her father's career and life in the military and so my thinking is that Larry was involved in little more than editing. He would know nothing about her Dad's life so he couldn't be involved in helping her write that part of the book. Of course he could do editing. Although she never spent a lot of time talking about the book I was very encouraging of her effort. I do know she was traveling to Arizona pretty regularly.

"If they were romantic why do you think they were travelling so far and so often to Arizona? They could have just as well stayed much closer to Santa Monica or Vegas."

"I'm not sure. But perhaps it was to fill in some details about the environment that she was raised in. But I can't vouch for that. Perhaps it provided her with a cover so her husband would not suspect any hanky-panky. May I ask you Detective, is he a suspect? Have you spoken to him?"

"I can't give you any details, as this is an ongoing investigation. Can you think of anything else that might be important about your ex client that might be helpful to us? Did she have close friends? Did she have any enemies?"

"She would pretty much do anything to avoid conflict since parental conflict was endemic to her childhood so I don't think she had any enemies. Madeline had learned to be obedient because of her strict militaristic father. She also learned she could do nothing about her parents' arguments. Her basic MO was to be friendly and non confrontive. My effort to have her write about her dad was designed to help her examine the MO that she had learned and which I knew was not helpful to her life. She was as deferential to her husband as she had been to her dad."

"But didn't she ever tell you about their fights?"

"Yes she would get fed up after a while and explode but she would always come back and beg for forgiveness. The fighting or confrontation scared her."

"Anything else that you can think of about her relationships that might be important?

"I know she had wanted to blog about politics. She was surprised that people would get upset. But I wouldn't know who they were and I think she stopped that shortly after she started.

"What else might be important for me to know, Dr. Milgram?

"Madeline had lots of girlfriends. One thing that I can be very sure of is that none of her girlfriends liked Gary." She repeated this very frequently.

"Why do you think she did that?"

"I think it was her way to show me that Gary was a bad guy and that her judgment as his wife wasn't the judgment of a bitchy wife.

"Is there anything else that you can think of that might be helpful?'

Jerry hesitated. There was another person he might name. The problem was the man was still married and any investigation might set off alarm bells for his wife.

"That was the first time you hesitated in this interview could you please tell me what you were thinking."

"It was an ex-boyfriend.Madeline would occasionally have a drink with him. As best as I could tell there was no hanky-panky going on between them. Madeline was pretty religious and so she did not want to contribute to the break up of a marriage

"Would you be able to tell me his full name?

"I would prefer you get it from her husband. I'm sure Gary can provide it to you

"How do you know he would know about this unnamed guy?"

"Because in one of their couple sessions Gary expressed anger and jealousy

"So you saw the two of them as a couple as well as her individually. Isn't that unusual?

"Yes it is but I am very comfortable and believe in that modality. Madeline wanted it, also thinking I could get through to Gary. Off the record, detective, I don't think I got through to him. He was deeply wrapped up in his own needs.

"Can you tell me what was said at that particular session? For the second time in the interview Jerry hesitated

"Gary said that he would murder them both if she ever saw James again. Jerry realized that he had let the name slip out. Zuma ignored it but Jerry realized that it would not be forgotten.

"Thank you Dr. Milgram. You've been very helpful. If I need to call upon you again I feel I can. At this point I don't feel I need to subpoena your notes or your emails."

"No, Detective Zuma, please subpoena them. If there ever were a question about my release of confidential information and it would be useful for me to show any authority that . I would like to have a record that you subpoenaed them. I would have to show the board that I just hadn't volunteered clients on my own. I need your formal request. But let me assure you that as much as possible I would like to be involved in helping you solve this case.

"I'm curious, Doctor. You almost seem eager to help. I know you are very busy so why take time out of your schedule? And I assume that you are also losing money.

"At this stage of my career money doesn't matter much. I mostly enjoy intellectual challenges. Working with police on crimes provides me with that kind of challenge. I have done things like this before. I enjoy being able to get out of the office and speak to people without identifying myself as a therapist, and I sometimes find it equally challenging as many of my cases. It's a break for me. And when the case is challenging it captures my attention. I guess I look at it as a kind of community service. So I guess for all those reasons, and maybe some others that I am not aware of, I would like it if you feel you can call upon me."

"Thank you, I may."

Zuma wondered if this guy would be more of a pain in the ass than help. He recalled the old joke from his AA meetings, which got repeated a lot. It seemed that in every meeting someone who would be telling their story would include references to a therapist who failed. That reference got lots of nods and "yeahs'. AA culture ridiculed traditional psychotherapy. Did you hear the one about the two psychologists who come across a man in the middle of the road who has been stabbed and is bleeding to death? And one turns to the other and says, 'let's find the person who did this.'

"I will send you a subpoena the moment I get back to my office. In case your notes don't have it, can you remember names of any and all girl or male friends that Madeline had? And include them in a return email.

"Sure"

"Thank you Dr. Milgram. Good-bye for now."

"I see the light is going on and my next patient is here. I'll have to say goodbye to you too."

Jerry had a few moments to reflect before opening the door for the next patient. It seemed that there were three suspects: The husband, Gary; the writer collaborator, Larry; and the ex-boyfriend, James. This seemed like a simple case but he also knew that like clients who seemed simple and direct in the beginning it often turned out to be the very opposite. He would wait to see if the case would seem simple or prove to be challenging. He recalled some of the names that Madeline had mentioned in her sessions that he had not put down in his notes, except with a first name. There were girlfriends and other members of Gary's family. Those additions, especially Gary's family, could easily make the case more complicated and interesting. Madeline had said that Gary's brother was a creep, was probably involved in drugs and he along with the mother in law hated Madeline. Creeps and hatred make for a good combination of possible suspects.

CHAPTER 14

Two days later as he left his office Jerry Milgram was met by a very tall, statuesque, blond male.

"If you are Dr. Milgram, I need to speak with you now." The words were delivered in a menacing tone and there was no question that this speaker was going to insist if not demand a response.

"Please tell me who I am speaking to."

"You don't know me .You've never met me before but I know that Madeline has mentioned my name."

Jerry became very cautious. He could talk about patients to detectives but not anyone off the street

"How might I be able to help you?"

The man started to scream. "You can mind your own goddamn business. Some detective showed up at my house poking around and asking questions and my wife got very suspicious. That didn't come out of the blue so I figured he must have gotten my name from you or from her dick of a husband."

"I can assure you that I had nothing to say to that detective that would put you in danger and I would appreciate you not speaking to me in the manner you are."

The statue screamed louder. "You'll appreciate it even less if you or that detective or anyone else shows up in my house asking questions and bothering my wife or me. Do you fucking understand me? You had better understand that I am for real." He abruptly turned and walked away.

Jerry entered his car, believing it must be James and began reflecting on the character he'd just met. 'People who are guilty of murder often get angry when they are confronted. He doubted whether Zuma had enough information to challenge or to confront him and was just trying to get information. Why was he so provoked? Was he guilty or was he just concerned that his wife might get upset? He did seem capable of violence as he was shouting and screaming in an office building and unafraid of what anyone might be hearing. Maybe he was just trying to get me in trouble with the landlord for having clients that would be making a ruckus and disturbing other tenants in the building'.

He wondered if he should call the detective but decided not to and went home. When he checked his messages, the detective had already called telling him that James had been pretty upset and was planning to speak to him. "Thanks a lot" he muttered to himself. Nothing like a warning that arrives too late. In this case 'late was much better than never. The contact would allow him to talk more with Zuma and perhaps get more involved in the case.

CHAPTER 15

Gary debated whether he should go to the drive in for his usual hamburger or to drop into his mom's. She would be happy to see him and happier to feed him. She had become unusually sweet to him since the death of his wife. Madeline didn't like her even before they met and they never got along. Madeline always complained that Gary was a mama's boy and therefore unfit to be a husband. She made fun of him saying that he was so attached that he consulted with his mother about business decisions as well as seeking advice about his marriage. From the beginning the relationship between Madeline and Mrs. Murray, Gary's mother, was bitter and full of shouting and even cuss words from his mom. Madeline had grown up in a household where no cuss words were ever used and she stopped using them after her father washed her mouth out with soap. The relationship between daughter and mother-in-law had never even approached civility. Gary was afraid that his mother would start with "Your lucky to be rid of her" comments but thought he would politely ask her to stop knowing that had never worked before. He was hopeful that his mother might be sensitive that despite all their arguments that he had had with Madeline that he still had lost his wife.

"God you are a sight for sore eyes" said his brother upon opening the door.

"Thanks bro you look like you've spent the day drinking?"

'Stop! Stop! Stop! I don't want the arguing between the two of you to begin the moment you see each other." For god's sake, the three of us are a family. We have no more in-laws to worry about. Let's get along."

Gary decided to let the in-laws comment pass. For his mom, that was an improvement on the cussing.

"I don't wanna argue mom, I just assumed that when there's been a murder the husband is the usual suspect . I was wondering how he was doing.

I figured Gary had to be scared chickenshit."

Gary lunged towards his brother but their mother was quicker with the big frying pan as she stepped between them.

"You both know I will use this if I have to. No more damn warnings."

"I may be getting my ideas from watching special victims units but that doesn't mean they're wrong".

"Maybe spending all day watching TV is good for you. At least it's better than spending all of your days in a bar. I wonder if you're ever going to grow up and do a hard day's work."

"I don't see you making a lot of money from all the hard work you're doing. Madeline always said you never charged enough especially to your friends and then you would drink it away on the way home. You're the sucker wasting time and money."

"Its my money and I earned it. Madeline always said that you were a leech, taking money from Mom, paying no rent and refusing to grow up. Probably baby leech would be a better way to describe you. I'll bet you got momma to pay for your car wash. It's cleaner than I have ever seen it. Did she also pay for your car buffing? And how do you get all your money for beer and weed? I know Momma wouldn't give you money for that? Are you getting your ideas from those creeps on your TV programs?"

Mrs. Murray swung her pan back and forth and hit each of her sons on the side of their head. They began to bleed. Her voice was very low.

"I told you. Now are you going to stop?" The boys became quiet and just glared at each other.

"Much better. Now I can make each of you tostadas and I can warm up some tortillas. Would that be OK??

"Sure mom, do you have a cold beer? I don't even know why I should ask. I'm sure if he's here all day with you watching TV there has got to be cold beer."

"Gary, I'll use the pan again on the other side of your head if you don't stop. Now, tell us, son, what is going on with your case? Do they have any suspects? Are they still bothering you?"

"I don't know mom. When the detective questioned me I told him I was asleep at home. I think I am no longer under suspicion."

"Well that's good for them to know. I know you had nothing to do with this."

"Yeah Mom, I know but I'm not sure they believe me."

"If you were sleeping alone bro and you have no one to verify your statement I don't think you' alibi will be worth much."

"I guess watching TV has helped you improve your vocabulary. "Verify...wow more than two syllables"

"And the m f word is four syllables and I'll precede it with an adjective dumb."

"You always loved cuss words. I guess that's because you stopped school in the eighth grade and that was the last time you ever learned anything, especially new words."

"Try these three words on for a murder, bro. Sex, money or power. That what's usually involved in a murder especially when a husband is involved with the murder of a wife."

Mrs. Murray couldn't use the pans as they were being used. She reached down searching for a big pot. Gary grabbed her hand. "Mom I will stop now. I promise you."

They were silent for the entire meal. The only sounds came from the six beer tops opening and the belches from the three of them.

On the way home Gary again wondered how Willie survived without ever seeming to have a job. He was always high when Gary showed up and he didn't think Mom would or could afford to support his habit. He brushed these thoughts aside. Madeline always said he was probably high on the booze that his buddies were probably giving him. Gary had given up wondering or worrying about his brothers' life.

As he pulled into his driveway he became anxious. Perhaps his brother was right and Zuma was still suspicious. How could he prove that he was innocent? How could they prove that he was guilty? His brother had taught him that in a murder investigation the police need a victim, a suspect, a weapon and a motive

They had a victim. His wife. They had a suspect. Him. He knows about a weapon, What motive could they attribute to him? He could not see that the motives that Harry had mentioned could possibly apply to him. There was no money that he gained from Madeline's murder. Even if Madeline had a lover he did not see himself as being the jealous type. And he saw no gain in his power by her death. He felt that he would be easily clear from prosecution. He suddenly remembered the words that he had uttered in Dr. Milgram's office. 'I would murder them both.'

CHAPTER 16

Detective Zuma was waiting for Gary when he pulled up to his house

'Mr. LaBelle, I know it's late at night and I am sorry if I disturbed you but I just have a few questions for you. Can you talk now?"

"Sure, Detective."

"Your wife's Porsche is only two years old and yet she has almost 160,000 miles on it. Can you explain why she would have done so much driving? That's a lot of mileage for two years."

"I'm not sure. I know she would drive at least once a month to Vegas with a girlfriend. Maybe it would be twice but that's about all I know about her driving."

"When she took it in for oil changes and check ups weren't you ever with her?"

"No, I asked her if she wanted me to join her but she always liked to do that herself.

"Did you ever wonder why she went so often? And why she preferred doing this on her own.? Women are usually at a big disadvantage in a garage repair shop."

"No, I never thought much about it. I knew she liked to hang around that garage. I thought it was because she loved her car. She didn't take care of our home but she took care of that damn Porsche."

"That's a pretty expensive car .Can you tell us how your wife could afford it?"

"I'm not sure. I think it might have been an advance from the publisher. She said they really like the idea of a Military hero. McCain was very popular so they thought the public would be interested. I think Madeline was hoping to get an endorsement from Senator

McCain. She said if she could get that it would help get an advance from a publisher."

Zuma knew that advances to unknown authors were very rare . He decided to ignore it.

"Did you ever notice any peculiar smells in the car?"

"That's a really weird question Detective. As I said that car was her pride and joy and she took care of it. What kind of smells were you thinking could be there?"

Zuma ignored the question. He thought Gary might have smelled marijuana but also realized that even if he had it wouldn't say much about Madeline that was important.

"If we calculated even two trips a month that would only be 13,000 miles a year. There's a lot of mileage to be accounted for. Can you give me the name of the girlfriend that she usually drove with and the one that she usually stayed with?

"Megan was the girl she drove with. I don't know the name of the girl she stayed with."

"Didn't she give you a number to call if something happens?"

"No, I had her cell and she never called."

"Can you give me the name and number of the garage she went to?"

"Sure."

Gary kicked himself when he realized that Zuma was going to find out about Madeline's driving record by asking questions to Megan and the garage people. He had wondered about the mileage also but whenever he brought it up Madeline had dismissed it. He didn't understand why the detective would want to bother with further questions about the mileage but realized it might be very important. He shivered as he thought about how negligent he had been to not realize that a once a month trip to Arizona would not get the mileage that she had made in the two years

"How could you be sure that when your wife told you that she was going to the garage, that in fact she went there?"

"I couldn't. If I called her and she picked up she could have been anywhere."

"OK Mr. LaBelle, thank you for your help. I'll be in touch with you if I need you to answer more questions."

This husband seems very cooperative but not at all informed about his wife's habits, friends or activities. Zuma wondered if it had always been that way with them or was it since Madeline had started working on the book with her dad. He and Carol had a locked in tight partnership that had not been weakened either by the passage of time or children. He smiles as he thinks of Carol's smile. She could light up a room. He never got tired of it. Carol's friends still called him. He turned most of the invites down. It seemed more painful to be with them and to be without Carol. He suddenly remembered that David was scheduled to have a big swimming meet for his college team. He wasn't sure if it was going to be held in Davis or where .He had better call Josh and set it up so the three of them could be there to cheer.

Gary wondered how the mechanic might be involved with Madeline?. Why would he want to kill Madeline?' What would he have to gain? . Money, power or sex were the three words that ran through his mind. The three words were followed by the sound of a church bell ringing in his head. It was the kind of ringing that told the hearer it was the end of an hour. Could Madeline have broken her marriage vows? Had her religious beliefs faded? He quickly passed over these questions. He didn't think he could discover anything about thinking about her or his relationship. Once he realized there were more suspects that needed to be interviewed the bell stopped ringing. After a few deep breaths he felt calm.

CHAPTER 17

"Does Megan Leavey live here?" He got her last name off the mailbox.

"This is detective Zuma. I have a few questions for you. It'll just take a few moments of your time .Can you please let me in?"

The door opened a crack. The chain held it in place. Zuma flashed his badge and the chain was unhinged. The apartment was in total disarray. It was late in the day and he imagined this girl liked to spend as much time as she could away from her apartment. He noticed a couple of whiskey bottles in the trash and an ashtray full of butts on the dining room table. Megan noticed the detective eyes glancing at the ashtray.

"Oh geez you're not gonna bust me for smoking. I know it's illegal to do it in apartments but I can't break the habit."

Zuma ignored her comment.

"Megan, how often did you travel with Madeline LaBelle?"

Megan paused. She had no desire to cooperate with the police and tell the truth to this detective but she also didn't want to lie.

"Can I ask you why you wanna know?"

"We're investigating a possible murder."

"Well how can I help you? I don't know anything about any murder."

"Madeline LaBelle was found dead near her car. We believe she was murdered."

"Oh my God I told her she should not be going to Vegas alone."

"So you used to travel with her to Vegas? How often did you do that?"

Megan realized she had given the detective what he had asked for

"It was twice a month. She needed to get away from that husband of hers and have some fun with me and another girlfriend. That husband was a royal pain to her. In Vegas we had a house that we could always stay in. We usually went to a few clubs and shows. Sometimes I would leave with a fellah. She never took anyone back to the house."

Zuma was surprised that Megan had revealed something about her single life but than realized that if she wasn't ashamed of the mess in her apartment why would sex with strangers in Vegas be something to be ashamed of.

"Do you have any of the names of the guys you left with?"

"I wouldn't ever bother getting to know their names. Why should I? I wasn't interested in them at all. I had a good time and that was enough. The only name I can give you was not from any one that I had been with. This guy kept calling me and asking when Madeline and was coming back to Vegas .I'm not sure how he got my number. I was always putting him off and then he started to ask for Madeline's number. He was pressing so hard and I gave him her cell phone.

"Can you check your phone to give me his phone number please? And do you know if Madeline ever heard from him."

"If she heard from him she never mentioned it to me. Here is his phone number. His first name is Jake."

"I have a few more questions. Megan do you know of anyone who would want to hurt Madeline?"

"Her husband was always angry with her for pretty much anything she did. It was a pain in the ass to be around them."

"Did you ever see them actually fighting?"

"I was driving once and I did see him put his hands on her neck. I pulled over and said I was going to call the police. Madeline said not to."

"And that was the only time you saw them in an actual fight?"

"Yes, but I always got an earful from her."

"Anyone else that you can think of that was angry at Madeline?"

"A couple weeks ago she said that her ex-boyfriend was trying to get back with her. She said he was pretty frustrated and annoyed that she wasn't willing to get back"

"And his name was?"

"James ."

"And the address and name of your Vegas girl friend??

"Lilly. Lilly Sears."

"Thank you Megan, you've been very helpful. Is there anything else that you think might be important for helping us find the murderer or murderers?"

"Yeah there was this thing that Madeline started about six months ago. She would insist on stopping at a place about halfway to Vegas. At first I thought it was a pee stop. But there was this one time when I had to go potty and when I got inside I saw her. She was in a booth with some guy. He was very good looking. I walked past and said nothing. When she came back in the car I asked her who it was and she said," a very old friend but I don't want to talk about it.' After that she stopped going to this diner and started going to a small family owned restaurant in Henderson for her so-called pee stop. This was weird to me because we were close to Lilly's house. She explained that it wasn't just a pee stop but it was too say a quick hello to the guy I had seen in the booth. She told me that his name was Phil. I guess she felt that her secret thing with this guy was not a secret anymore. But every time she left that restaurant her eyes were bloodshot. I didn't want to know about what she might be doing. But I didn't think it was good.

"Do you think you can remember what the address was?"

"No . But I remember where it was."

"Megan, I'm going to ask you to allow someone from my office to drive you out to Henderson. My assistant is Pat Vasquez and he will call you and take you there."

"Why do I have to do that? I really don't want to be involved."

"I could make you do it but it would be easier for you and us if you volunteered to help."

Megan figured the four or five hours of her time would be worth having any suspicions dropped and not to be bothered anymore. She also hoped that Pat was younger and cuter than Joe Zuma.

As Zuma drove home he thought he could eliminate Megan as a suspect in the Madeline murder but who was this Phil character, the vic from the hotel in Santa Monica? The restaurant seemed a bit close to the Lyons home. Why would he take that chance of being seen by his wife or colleagues from work? Lovers do all kinds of stupid things. Bloodshot eyes plus stupid things usually meant drugs.

The unanswered mileage was still a big puzzle. He was unsure about Gary's alibi and he could not rule out James as a suspect. And now there was a new character, Phil .A big piece of the puzzle was Madeline's mileage. Maybe the answer could be found by a visit to the girlfriend in Vegas or to the garage.

CHAPTER 18

The garage only had two forklifts. It was a small operation but had a very nice office for the walk-ins.

"Yeah, she liked coming here. Our place is air conditioned and clean and she could do whatever she was doing on her phone or computer. And I always liked it cause I liked looking at her. I made a few passes but she always turned me down. Gave me a bit of a lecture on her being married and how I needed to respect that. Shit detective, if I respected that I would never have any fun in this work. Women who bring their cars in are usually alone, divorced, widowed or separated. Since they are without a fellah the pickings are pretty good for me."

"Did you ever wonder about the amount of miles she was putting on her car?"

"Sure, I asked a couple of times. She was working on a book about her dad and was driving to Arizona a lot to get background. When she came in she brought a couple of notebooks. I think one must have been about Gary's business since it had lots of numbers in it. I think the other must have been the book she was working on."

"Did she always come in alone?"

"No, there was one time when she brought in some guy that she said was helping her write the book. They seemed pretty palzi walzie together. I thought her lectures on marriage were hollow so I kept trying."

"Do you know his name?"

"No."

"Did you think that there was something romantic between them?"

"I don't know. The drive to Arizona can be long and very boring. There are a lot of motels along the way. I assume that any guy could not help trying something with Madeline. She was a looker. Other clients who came in while she was sitting in the office were always trying to strike up a conversation with her. She shook them off and kept her attention to the work she brought with her. Even if the guys were given a cold shoulder they kept asking about her."

"Did you know what she was working on?"

"NO but I did notice it had to do with lots of numbers. Kind of like a ledger."

"Did you ever give out her number?

The mechanic laughed. "No, Detective, why in hell would I want to have competition?"

Zuma drove away not having any warm fuzzies for the owner of the shop but thinking how nice that in America there are these small singly owned shops where personal service is given and there is no corporation looking over your shoulder telling you what you must charge for this or that. They were the last of a dying breed. Even though he knew that women were more at a disadvantage in this small shop, as compared to a chain, he made a promise to himself that he would look for that kind of garage back in Santa Monica. And even if it was inconvenient because of distance or even more expensive he felt it important that he support a dying breed.

CHAPTER 19

The house in Vegas was probably 3,000 square feet. There was nothing about it that made it stand out since all the other houses were large and expensive. It was just another house in this posh suburb. Whoever had bought it or was paying the rent was spending big bucks. Joe thought it ironic that since all these expensive homes looked alike that they seemed like tract homes.

As messy as Megan was in appearance and furnishings, Lilly Sears was the opposite. The entrance and living room were immaculate. Zuma could spot nothing out of place. It almost seemed like no one lived there.

It was noon and she was dressed up as if she was going out for the evening.

"Thanks for meeting me with Ms. Sears. I got your name and phone number from your girlfriend in Santa Monica and I assume she called and told you what my visit would be about."

"Yes, she did and she told me your name and that you would be calling on me and that you were good looking for your age."

Zuma smiled. This woman knew her way around men.

"Ms. Sears. How did you hear about the death of Madeline?"

"Well, as I just said, Megan told me and when I asked about where she said that her body was found in Santa Monica."

Zuma took it in realizing he had told no one about where the body was found.

Did Megan know? If he hadn't said anything how did Sears know?

Lilly realized she had given the detective something that she wasn't supposed to know. She recovered quickly.

"The day after Megan told me about the murder I heard on this mornings news that a woman's body was found in Santa Monica I kind of figured it was Madeline's."

"I see."

Zuma thought not only did this gal know her way around men she was quick on her feet. He didn't think that a Las Vegas newscast would carry anything about a Santa Monica murder or a discovered woman's body. They had enough local news about murders, unknown corpses and missing people to keep their channels busy.

"Lilly, may I call you by your first name? Can you tell me about your relationship with Madeline.

"Yes, you can call me Lilly. All my friends do. Maybe that's where this relationship can move. You know, Joe, more of a friendship type thing."

Zuma did not respond. She was not going to be intimidated by his status as a detective. Zuma thought she knew her way around police investigations. He would not call her Lilly from now on.

"You were going to tell me about your relationship with Madeline."

"Oh my god, Joe. We go back so many years. We met in high school and we partied together. When I got married and moved to Vegas I didn't have any contact with her. Then about two years ago I received a phone call from her and she said she would like to visit. By then I was divorced. I got this house in my settlement and I was happy to hear from her. How awesome it was to reunite and have her come out and visit."

"How often did she visit?"

"I would say twice a month but sometimes it was only once a month."

"And she would stay with you?"

"Of course. My home is quite spacious. We have three large bedrooms. They all have their own full bathrooms. My bedroom is special. I would love to show it to you." She paused. "Would you be interested?"

Joe ignored the invitation. There was nothing shy or demure about this gal. She was determined to undermine the investigation.

"For us it must have been like having sleepovers in high school all over again."

"Yeah, but I would guess that it was much less crowded."

"And what would you do during the weekend?"

"We're both party girls. Actually all three of us are party girls. Megan would often come with Madeline."

Joe knew the next question would be personal but with a gal like Lily he was not hesitant to ask.

"And when the three of you party girls went out on the weekends how did you all end up?"

"It varied, Joe. I'm sure you would understand."

Zuma thought she was not going to give up on the more than a friendship thing.

"Sometimes I would bring a fellah home. If Megan was going to leave she would usually go with the guy to his place. Madeline never brought anyone home with her or went to anyone's place. She always ended up here."

"Was there any one club or hotel that was your favorite?"

"No we tried to make sure we got to all the big ones. They had the big spenders and we often got dinner."

"Did any of the guys you brought home express an interest in Madeline?"

"Joe, my history with Madeline is that if the two of us are ever out together the guys zoom in for her first so I try to keep some of my dates away from her, at least the ones I liked. I can also say that most of the guys I really didn't care for so it didn't matter to me if they expressed interest in Madeline in the morning."

"Do you know if she ever was responsive?"

"No, even though she is or I guess it's now **was** pretty unhappy married to that baby, Gary, she was not the kind of gal who would fool around."

Zuma heard the phrase "unlike you "run around in his head but kept silent.

"Can you tell me if Madeline used drugs?"

Lilly laughed." Oh, Joe, we all smoked pot before we went out, but I never saw her use anything besides that. If guys offered she would turn them down."

Zuma, decided to counter the chatty, informal level that Lilly had sought.

"Ms. Sears, I know you said you got this lovely home in a settlement but it looks like it would be quite expensive to keep up and the furniture looks high end."

"I'm a working girl, Joe. I push drinks at one of the best Hotels in Vegas .I get really good tips and that's why I'm dressed up now .All of us have to show up before we start working to make sure our skirts are short and our tits are hanging out. We're also drilled about who sells the most drinks. A monthly reward is given to one of the 25 gals who work there and I'm usually at the head of the line."

"Ms. Sears I don't want you to get dinged for being late for work but can you tell me if you know of anyone who might want to hurt Madeline."

"I know she got a lot of phone calls while she was here from her ex-boyfriend and when she got off the phone she was pretty upset and sometimes seemed frightened. But she didn't want to talk about it. Of course if I had to bet money on it, and in Vegas you can find someone who will make any kind of a bet, I'd put my chips on

'Gary. This other guy named Jake began calling about two weeks ago asking when Madeline was coming back. I kept telling him I didn't know. He made me promise to call him when she did. I said I would. I never got the chance but wouldn't have done it without Madelines' permission."

"Can I get Jake's number from you?"

"Sure, Joe. Are you sure that there's nothing else I can do for you?

Zuma smiled. 'She is relentless. No wonder she sells the most drinks'.

On the trip back to LA Zuma asked Pat to check and see if any of the TV stations in Vegas had reported the location of a woman's body in Santa Monica. When he got to his office Pat reported that there had been no Vegas TV stations reporting on Santa Monica murders or discovered bodies. It was just as Zuma had thought. They had enough garbage to deal with in their own city and had no need to report the doings in any other town. Didn't Vegas have the tenth highest murder rate for cities in America? People don't like crime but they don't get involved in comparing their cities murder rates to others. Comparisons don't make citizens feel lucky if their crime rate is lower. But how would Lilly Sears know that.

CHAPTER 20

The weekend with his sons had gone very well. Even though the University of California, Davis(UCD) lost to the University of California, Los Angeles, (UCLA)in the swim meet, Josh came in first in the 200-meter breast and butterfly strokes. David had arrived in time to scream his support and hurrahs. . The celebration afterwards, when the boys devoured a massive amount of food, cheered Joe. He always enjoyed feeding them knowing that they would at this age, still stay lean. Josh had reported that his paddle boarding in the Pacific had reached the point where he felt confident that he could take Joe out on the paddle board next summer at the cape.

"I'll be racing beside you while you pull dad along."

"Let's hope for your sake he doesn't put on a few more pounds."

The news that both boys were planning to return to the cape was the topper to the evening.

Now he was back at home and feeling relaxed and nostalgic. Joe did something that he had never told anyone about. It had started after Carol was killed.

He turned on his computer and began listening to Randy Newman sing "I think it's gonna rain today" He hadn't quite figured out why it meant so much to hear those words. After listening to Newman sing he began listening to the other versions and interpretations of Newman's song. Barbara Streisand, Joe Cocker and Bette Middler had all recorded this song with its sad, dark words. The version that struck the deepest chord of sadness in him was the one by Nina Simone. He marveled at the genius of Newman but also how these other talented folks could take that genius and do something that would not detract from the original but would add and be different.

He mulled over the words trying to figure out why they meant so much to him.

"A pale dark moon in a sky streaked with grey" was what he had often loved seeing in the heavens.

The irony of "Human kindness is overflowing" is what he knew about his world of work where human kindness was limited by greed and the hunger for power.

He knew as the song kept repeating that it was always going to rain. The rain would not stop. There is no need to be surprised. "I think it's gonna rain today.

The fake smiles of the murderers he had caught were like the "frozen smiles of the scarecrows that chased love away".

He listened to Simone's rendition for five times .Her singing the last word "Lonely" made him think of Carol. He loved this private time. He knew that Carol was the embodiment of the words;

"Bright before me, the signs implore me, help the needy and show them the way." Carol had been the one who convinced him that he was helping and protecting the needy and the innocent .He would do this knowing that "It's gonna rain today."

He shut the computer. "Good night darling. Thank you for everything. I still love you." He put out the lights knowing that it would be raining tomorrow.

CHAPTER 21

"Hi boss. It sure is a honey of a day."
"Yeah but I think it's gonna rain today."
"Huh?"
"Forget that Pat. Just talking to myself."
"Boss; I think you could use some coffee?"
"No thank you, Pat. I think I could use something stronger but I guess it will have to wait."

Zuma knew that his assistant took this as a joke. They were both in AA. Zuma had hit bottom after a hit-and-run driver had killed his wife. They were never able to find the driver but that was not because of anything that Zuma did. Everyone in the office believed that Zuma had lost it when he started to track down every driver in Los Angeles who had a DUI for the past three years . He tried to make account for their whereabouts on the night she was killed. It was during this time that his heavy drinking began. When he was asked to take a leave of absence or go on sick leave for three months he realized that his job was in jeopardy. It was then that he began his AA meetings. The meetings helped him realize that most hit-and-run drivers would not have a record. He was shocked to realize how dumb he had been. He had gone to meetings for ten years but now he no longer attends. He felt in control of his drinking

Pat had also gone to AA meetings but he had been more involved with Alanon. His father had been drunk and abusive and he had to learn to stay out of the way. He realized after a while he could not make his mother move out. He was, like his boss, more accepting of the world and what life handed you.

"Pat, this case keeps opening up more and more doors. This Lilly gal may not be a likely candidate for the murder but she has some connection to what happened.

Let's run a check on Sears, find out everything you can about her!! DUI s? Drug arrests? Anything? Also check out the divorce and the settlement please.

I think it was filed in Vegas."

"Sure boss."

As he drove home he wondered which suspect he would place his chips on.

Before calling it a night Zuma checked his emails.

There was that damn ad for the Viking cruises. He thought they were one god damn shrewd company. They had figured how never to let anyone unsubscribe. He had been trying every day for months. And no matter what he did he could never unsubscribe. He wondered if it would be a waste of time to write a letter. Viking would probably not respond. A lot of people would have to get pissed off and probably sign a petition or something and send it to a newspaper or have Rachel Maddow do a 'worst thing of the day' show. The other items in the email were mostly about the latest news when he saw what he was hoping for.

He had obtained permission to dig up Madeline's remains, since Gary had buried his wife without an autopsy. Pat had sent something with the subject matter of 'See This' .

The" See This "email had six attachments. There were mugshots of Lilly sears with DUIs; One from two years ago; the other ten years ago; a court document indicating a plea of guilty to a charge of possession and selling of cocaine ;and a newspaper article reporting a non guilty verdict for a trial on prostitution. The divorce papers indicated no contest with an even split of assets of about $150,000. Not nearly enough to get her into that fancy house, thought Zuma.

The final attachment had what he hoped for. Her fancy Vegas had been purchased and registered to her and a man named Ivan Licht.

So Ms. Sears, you're a working girl but it looks like you've had some other jobs outside of your hard days' work. Drugs, prostitution,

D U I s And who was Licht. Ivan is a Russian name. Russian mafia? Drugs? Did Madeline know any of this? Sears had to know the "I'm just a working girl "con would only work for so long. If she was seriously involved with drugs she would know that his visit would be followed up with a warrant to search her home. Zuma knew that the moment he left she would start to clean out her home of hidden drug money or drugs. If Licht was involved she would have called him.

Before he opened the last attachment he called Pat.

"Get a judge in Vegas to issue a warrant to search Lilly Sears' house."

"On what grounds, boss?"

"For Christ's sake, Pat. I don't know. Make it up if you have to. Tell the judge I saw cocaine in her bedroom when I was doing a routine investigation. And check with all the banks in Vegas if any large deposits had come in from her. I know she's probably smart enough not to do that but do it anyway. Also check for wire transfers in her name or the name Ivan Licht . Yes that's a shitload of work. That's what we do. And I'm going to take you to a two hour drive out of town with someone who may lead us to a brand new suspect, named Phil. Watch out for Megan…. She smokes and drinks and I think she is on the make.

"Sure Boss. Give me her number. I'll call her right after I get hold of a Vegas judge."

The email from the morgue medical examiner confirmed that Madeline had been shot twice in the chest and that was the cause of death. The bullets were from a Glock 35. There were needle marks on her legs and left arm.

So the sweet, friendly, proper, Mrs. Labelle has no enemies but is a druggie. If she were doing any kind of business with drugs she would have to have enemies. As Zuma turned off the overhead light next to his bed he mused that the next few days would be visiting days for Pat and for him. . As he dozed off he wondered what the police may have found in trying to trace the bullets and what Gary would say when he was told about his wife's drug use and asked why he said nothing about the drug use to Zuma.

CHAPTER 22

"Gary, when did you realize your wife was using drugs? And how come you never mentioned that to me before."

"I couldn't believe it when I saw all the needle marks. I felt ashamed. I didn't see any need to tell you. She was dead."

"Before I go ahead Gary I want you to tell me everything you didn't tell me in our first visit. The neighbors indicated a very different story about your relationship. You may want to call a lawyer. I don't think you realize you're a major suspect in this case."

"Oh my god. My fucking brother is right.

"Huh?"

"OK, Detective. Madeline and I fought. We fought a lot. She bit me and scratched me and the police were called in quite often. I was angry about her trips. She was leaving every weekend for about two years. When I pressed her about it she said it was none of my business but she had to get away from my stupid eating and drinking and watching sports on T.V." She said she was bored with me. She never understood how hard I was working. I didn't hire extra help so I would earn more money. In the beginning I would give it all to her. But it never was enough. After a while I began spending it on the way home drinking with my friends and she bitched more about how little I was making and what a lousy businessman I was."

Zuma felt sorry for the guy. It probably was a match that could never work.. Gary was a simple hard working guy who never imagined what could be in life. He had entered a world where people worked, drank and did little beyond going bowling, traveling to Vegas, or eating out. Madeline had aspirations that her father had probably instilled in her about the world and different cultures. They were too young, too naïve and it was doomed from the beginning. He and Carol had also been young, and naïve. Zuma realized they had been 'lucky.

Zuma thought 50 or so trips to Vegas a year might explain the mileage but would not explain what the trips were for. Megan said that she went about once a month or so and Lilly had indicated that Madeline came out once every two months or so. So maybe, the trips to Vegas or elsewhere meant that Madeline was involved in buying and dealing drugs.

"Gary, did you notice that Madeline had begun to spend money in the past year?"

"I did. When I asked her about it she said she had received a cash advance on her book."

"Did she tell you how much?"

"No. But I know she gave $30,000 to that guy she works with."

"How do you know that? Was it in cash?"

"She left a big envelope on her desk with his name on it. When I got up early in the morning before she woke up I looked inside. I counted it. I couldn't believe it. I had never seen so much money in my life. I counted it twice. There were 300, 100 dollar bills. All the bills were crisp and clean. It was easy to count but it took me a long time. I forgot the numbers as I counted so I had to start putting them in piles of 50 each."

"Did you ask her about why she was giving 30 grand to this guy?"

"I did. She called my stupid and asked me if I forgot that he works with me on the book. I didn't know anything about books so I just assumed she was telling me the truth. And I figured if she gave him thirty she would have more than that for herself. I guess I was also hoping it would be for us. I don't know where the other thirty might be."

"Tell me where you were on the night before you received the phone call from the police indicating they found her body.

It was one of the longest pauses that Zuma had ever seen a suspect take.

"OK this is the part I didn't tell you about. I didn't go to work that day. I was determined to find out where she was going. I followed her all the way to Vegas. She made about three stops at different homes and stayed only a few minutes in each home. She went to dinner on the Strip and I walked in on her and asked her what she had been doing. At first she said that it was none of my business. After we argued some more she said that she was meeting with possible agents for her book. I knew that was b.s. I told her that agents would want to spend more than three minutes with her. She got angry and asked me to leave. I told her no. I told her we were going to drive back together and see Dr. Milgram as soon as he was able to see us. She laughed at me and started repeating that stuff about how I was boring and not a good businessman. She also said she didn't want to waste her time seeing Milgram because she was going to get a divorce. I couldn't believe those words. I became furious but was able to hold back. I begged and begged her to drive back with me. I thought a car ride together might calm her down and I could easily arrange to have her car driven back. She did calm down and said that she wouldn't leave with me but I could follow her in my car. I did that. We stopped after about an hour and half for coffee. We were both exhausted. I followed her on the freeways and when we got on the 405 she signaled that she was getting off. She pulled into a diner and I followed her in where she ordered some pasta. I went to the bathroom while she was eating and when I came back she was gone. Her car was still in the parking lot so I figured she couldn't get very far on foot. I asked a driver in the lot if he had seen any one coming out of the diner and the guy said a woman took off in a car with a guy she seemed to know. The guy said the driver had waved to her and she just hopped in and they took off like a bat out of hell. I tried to follow and guessed that they might be heading towards the freeway. No luck. I didn't know what kind of car to look for so I headed back to the diner and began making the rounds of places, bars and restaurants that she had mentioned but had no luck. I gave up after two hours of searching for her and went home to bed.

Zuma sighed, believing that he could now at least eliminate one suspect. He always felt good when a suspect would no longer be under suspicion. And he was glad that Gary was not the murderer. He was either dumb or emotionally blind. Another guy who could not keep up with a very smart wife,

"Gary, Madeline was shot twice in the chest. They are now tracing the bullets back hoping to find the registered owner of the gun."

"Why are you telling me that?"

"Gary do you own a gun?"

"Yes I do."

"Can I see it?"

"I don't have it. The morning I got the news about Madeline's body and seeing her needle marks, I decided I didn't ever want to be around violence. I walked down to the ocean, waited for low tide, dug a hole that must have been two feet deep and buried it. I sat there and waited for the tide to come in to make sure it was gone."

"You waited six hours?"

"Yup."

"Did anyone see you? We can check with a lifeguard if you were there."

Yes, a lifeguard came over and asked me if I was OK. I told him my wife had been murdered. He was shocked and just walked away.

Zuma would tell Pat to check with the lifeguard on duty but also believed that Gary was telling the truth. It would be too easy to find out if he was lying. Zuma was back at square one. Rather than go home he thought he would head to Vegas. Hopefully Pat had got the warrant to search Silks house. Unlike the other visitors to Vegas he didn't give much hope for being successful.

CHAPTER 23

The house in Vegas had been cleaned out. Silk had left in a hurry. All the drawers and closets were open. The fridge door was also open with some smelly cheese. Zuma called the hotel where she worked.

"She called in to say she was leaving town for a long holiday and that we should hold on to her pay checks. She would let us know where she was living so we could mail them to her. It was just a message so I didn't have a chance to ask her anything."

"Did you call her to find out anything? When she might come back?"

"Sorry Detective, I don't babysit anymore. If I played social worker to all the gals who worked here I would never get any work done. They all need social workers but we're running a hotel not a halfway house."

When he drove over to check the Ivan Licht house the neighbors say he had left with a lady and her car seemed to have lots of things in it.

He decided to ask the police to put out an all points bulletin once Pat could get the license plate and vehicle type from the Nevada DMV for Karen's car. He called the Vegas police and asked them to impound Lichts car looking for drugs or weapons. He also realized that by the time the all points bulletin was in effect they could be in Mexico. He felt stymied and drove slowly back to his office.

He parked in the half full parking lot and sat in his car thinking. It was a cloudless night and for a change stars were visible. Seeing the stars made him realize how little he could see about the killer or killers in this case. This time the space did not bring peace but was a reminder that he was lonely. Speaking to Pat might help. He was comparing the stars off Cape Cod and Santa Monica when he realized that he hadn't asked Gary for any of the addresses of Madeline's stops. He imagined that Gary might remember where he went, but if he was just following her it was unlikely. He hoped that Gary would remember and, if so, a tale began to develop in his head.

Zuma went over the scenario of the case in his head. If Madeline was involved with Silk in scoring drugs and selling them in L.A. she would drive out to Vegas, every week, pick them up from Silk or Licht or maybe both. Megan was a cover for her to hide from Gary what was going on. Maybe Madeline had started to get unhappy with the arrangement and started to skim? Or maybe she and Silk or even Licht had an argument? That always has seemed a likely scenario whenever drug money was involved. There seemed to be a ton of 'don't knows'. Each of them played out in his mind . They were like the bulletins on a TV show where a talking head was speaking but you watched the bulletins.

We **don't know** who was the person who killed Phil Lyons. Suspects are Madeline,Mrs. Lyons,Gary.

We **don't know** who was the person who showed up in Santa Monica at the diner whisking Madeline away. Suspects? Gary,Larry, Licht,; but had to be someone she knew and felt comfortable with.

We **don't know** who killed Madeline. Suspects? Gary, Larry, Licht.

We **don't know** if Gary's alibi will stand up. .

We **don't know** where James fits in the picture.

We **don't know** about the unanswered mileage.

We **don't know** if and how Madeline sold drugs?

We **don't know** what was going on with Madeline's manuscript? Where the hell was Larry the collaborator in all of this? Did he have any thing to do with drugs, or the murder?"

A big piece of the puzzle that needed to be solved was why Madeline had so much mileage? Maybe the answer to that could be found by a visit to the girlfriend in Vegas or to the garage.

Did Gary own the gun they were now trying to trace? Did he really bury it in the sand? His head was bursting and he thought about the gun that Gary said he had buried. Right now he wished he could put his head into some cool, wet sand. He called Pat.

"Yes, boss, the all points bulletin will be released shortly. The car has been impounded and they found traces of cocaine and H."

"Can you have the Redondo police run their metal detector on the beach looking for a gun that Gary said he buried."

"That sounds kind of desperate, Boss."

"No. I'm not desperate. They have done it before. We do it all the time here in Santa Monica. Favorite burial spot is under the pier. Make an appointment with him and ask him to show you where he buried it. If he can't remember make sure the metal detector crew checks the Redondo pier at low tide."

"Sure boss."

"O.K Pat, listen to me. This is what we are pretty sure of. We got information that there is 30,000 grand in cash… clean bills so probably drug money, a gangland style murder, a confirmed druggie, suspects leaving town and an impounded car with evidence of coke use. Clear picture. Eh? Zuma wrote them all on the wall. Under 'Knowns' he wrote all the questions that were in his head when he sat in the parking lot. The 'Don't knows' occupied a much larger space than the Knowns.

"Boss we have seven unknowns but they're not equal in importance. I think we're definitely closing in."

But Pat was right; they didn't need to know all the unknowns to solve the case.

"Pat which if them is the most important to you?"

"The last person who saw or was with Madeline. That's either Gary or the one who drove her away. Another unknown"

"I agree. And which is the one that seems least important?

"The collaborator and the script.

"I agree again. Let's go visit Mr. Collaborator and find out as much as we can about this script and the advance and the publishing company,

Pat smiled. He felt he had helped his boss get focused and indeed when Zuma left to go home for the night the stars seemed brighter, and for a moment he could smell the Pacific Ocean breeze and imagined he was back at the cape. He would have a peaceful night. He just needed to keep digging the way the metal detector people w do.

CHAPTER 24

As Jerry Milgram was driving to work on Monday, because the line to get off the freeway was moving slowly he decided he could safely check his phone messages. There were two.

"Dr. Milgram, We have never met. My name is Larry Kimball. I was working with Madeline on her book and I need to come in and speak with you. I know this is unusual but I am willing to pay you for your time. Please call me back as soon as you can."

"Dr.Milgram, this is Gary, Madelines' husband. I need to come in and see you as soon as possible. Please call me back and I will make sure I can come in when you have an opening".

Jerry smiled. He had wondered what had happened to the case and felt badly that his services were not being utilized. Maybe these two calls would help get him into the mystery of Madelines' murder and end his feeling of neglect.

"Hi Gary, This is Dr. Milgram. I'm returning your call. How are you doing?"

"I'm very upset. It's not only the loss of my wife, it's knowing that she was murdered, knowing she was left on the road, seeing her in the morgue. I'm regretting everything I had ever said to her that I knew could hurt her. And of course I feel stupid. I can't get over that she was using drugs and that I never knew it."

"Gary, addicts are excellent at hiding things. They do it full time. And I do mean full time, night and day. That's why when there is an addict or a murderer on the loose, you can bet they have thought a lot about everything related to what they are doing or have done. That's why we need detectives. Gary, what can I help you with?

Jerry thought that Gary would want to talk about how to grieve so he was taken aback with his next comment.

"I hid my gun. I stupidly hid it" I can't believe how stupid I am."

Jerry's antennae became laser-like and went forward. If Gary were to confess to the murder he would have to report him. He did not want to be accused in court of prying things out of his client.

"Tell me what you mean you "hid your gun"

"I became nervous about having my gun in my house. All that violence just upset me and I was afraid I might use it. So I just went out to the Redondo pier and buried it at low tide."

Jerry was careful to paraphrase. "Are you saying that in this investigation of your wife's death that you never used your weapon?"

"Right."

"So why are you calling me. Do you want to see me?"

"I'm not sure. I'm scared. I know that the detective doesn't believe me. If they don't find the weapon I think he will still go after me. My brother says the husband is always the key suspect in a murder. I feel like that detective is like a locomotive heading straight towards me and I can't get out of his way"

Jerry was surprised that Gary was able to conjure up the metaphor. I guess fear can contribute to creativity.

"Can you speak to the detective? Tell him that I came to see you and told you the absolute truth that I had nothing to do with the shooting."

Gary could hardly hold back from laughing.

"Even if you gave me permission to talk to him I cannot vouch for the truth of what you are telling me."

"But you know that the most violent thing I did was to hit her. You know me."

"I know you but only slightly. But I also know that most of us are capable of murdering people we love, especially if we feel we have been hurt. Would you want to talk more about that to me?"

"How do you think that would help?"

"It usually helps people who are upset or afraid or anxious to talk to another person. You could try and see if that works for you."

"I already told the detective how I followed Madeline to Vegas and watched as she visited three houses and I walked in on her as she was dining and begged her not to divorce me and to have us go back to therapy with you. I thought she was going to do that and we stopped at a diner in Santa Monica. We ordered and I went to the John. When I got back she was gone. I tried looking for her. Some guy in the parking lot said that this gal had come running out of the diner. A car pulled up, the driver opened the door and she jumped in. The guy said she seemed to know the driver and they just took off. My last moment with her was in the diner when we both ordered pasta. Honest Dr. Milgram, that was the last I saw her and after that I buried my gun."

"Did you ask her about her stops in Vegas?"

"I did and she said something about seeing agents for her book. I didn't believe her and she got angry. I never found out why she was there."

"Do you know anything about her manuscript? Has her collaborator contacted you?"

"Yes, he has but I haven't got back to him."

Jerry thought there would be some legal haggling about rights to the sales

"Gary, you might want to speak to a good contract lawyer to see about your rights or entitlements to future sales of Madeline's book. But right now you don't know if the manuscript is close to finishing and who is going to finish it."

"If I had my way it would never get published. That's what I wanted."

"I know but you may not be able to stop it. You need to see a lawyer. I can recommend one for you if you would like."

"Dr. Milgram, do you see anything I can do to help solve this murder?"

"I think you just keep on telling your truth."

"My brother says, the truth doesn't always matter and since I don't have a good alibi, it looks to them that I am guilty. I hid my gun, but if it is never found, me, the husband, is the most likely to be brought to trial."

Jerry knew that Gary was repeating what he had said earlier but that he was right.

"You're just going to have to believe in our justice system. And if Zuma asks me about you and you give me permission I will tell him you were both anxious about seeming guilty and eager to help with any aspects of the investigation. And you might want to do your best to find your gun. If you find it before they do it will make you look good in their eyes.

"That's a good idea. Thanks Dr. Milgram. I'll keep you posted if I have any luck finding the gun. I feel better after talking with you. Maybe I will come in to speak directly with you.

"My door is always open for you, Gary."

Jerry believed that Gary's anxiety was real. He did not know if it was based on his lack of faith in the criminal justice system or because he had actually murdered his wife. He felt slightly defeated, as he did not have any new information or ideas that would lead to the solving of this case. Maybe, Larry, the collaborator, might help Jerry, the therapist collaborate with Zuma.

CHAPTER 25

"Hi Mr. Kimball. This is Dr. Milgram returning your call. I'm happy to chat with you. Would you like to make an appointment?"

"No, I'm not sure. I want to talk with you about the manuscript I was working on with Madeline."

"Let me understand this Mr. Kimball. You don't want to seek therapy or counseling but want advice as to what to do with the manuscript. I'm not the one you should speak to about that. I think a lawyer would be more appropriate."

"I guess you're right about that but don't you work with writers. Madeline said you did. I know you worked with her on our manuscript."

"Yes I have a practice that includes writers."

"Well then can I come in and see you?"

"Oh so you would want to come in to discuss the substance of the book?"

"Yes."

"Sure I can do that. Would this Friday at three work for you? Do you think we will need more than one hour?"

"I don't think so."

"O.K. See you then. If you have any questions about the address and the like you can Google me."

Jerry hung up. Kendall sounded as if he was making it up in order to see him. He doubted that it was for advice about writing. Jerry's curiosity was wetted. This guy was clearly lying, and wanted to hide something or get Jerry to believe or do something. The collaborator might be his way into the case so he could collaborate more closely and work with Zuma.

CHAPTER 26

Immediately upon passing through customs at the Mexico-U.S. border Ivan turned to Lilly.

"This is what we are going to do .You are going to have to trust me. First, we need to sell our car. Will take it to a chop shop. Second, we found a motel. From there we are going to get new driver's licenses, and buy a used car You're going to get your hair done differently. I'm going to get an expensive wig, one that doesn't look like a wig.

Lilly was impressed. He had clearly thought through what needed to be done. She liked that about him. When Ivan was doing business he did business and the order of the steps that needed to be taken was very clear.

"Once we get to our motel I will call my connections to find out when they can see me. They'll want to know why I didn't make the wire transfer and meet my L.A. supplier. I'll tell him why I'm on the lamb and . I will have to let the L.A. guy know that we will not be in contact with him for a few weeks and that he should not try to contact me. Nothing has been proven but we don't want to deal with coppers. You understand why I don't want you to know whom I deal with. It's better for you that you know nothing. I will tell them and it will be less worrisome to them. They'll be glad that I have found someone else to deal with. I have no doubts they'll be able to give business to the guy who was my connection and worked for them. Right after I leave you you're going to call our connection in L.A. and explain to him why I didn't meet with him last night. Tell him it's going to take us a month or so before we can be back in business.

You don't need to know his name. I'm just giving you a number and leaving a message. Preface it with "Ivan and I"

You and I have enough money to enjoy the beaches and bars. Also they've got a gambling joint in town. If you wanted to work I'm sure that they would love a gringa supplying drinks. If you get a job there you travel with Uber. Do not use the car we purchase. Got it?"

She looked at Ivan. He was very confident. It was clear to Lilly that he knew his way around this town.

"I don't want a flea bitten hotel. You better get one next to some place where I can get a pedicure, hair wash and coloring."

"I gotcha. I know the perfect place. And a few doors down is where you can do all your beauty stuff. It's going to take me some time to get real good fake drivers licenses. We'll probably have to go back to get them unless they are not crowded and I can just wait. Now this is important. When I drop you off at the motel this is what we do first. We have to make sure the cash is in a safe place. We're going to put it in the toilet, in a plastic bag. Keep out a grand for the licenses, $2000, for a used car, and for spending money another five. I'll pay 2,000 in cash to the motel so he won't come knocking on our door and will leave us alone. We should have over 170,000 left to start up again. You pee in the toilet so that if anyone looks in there they will not think anything is in the water. Put some toilet paper on top of the plastic bag so the cash doesn't show. We'll tie a string around the bag in case someone flushes the toilet, so the bag won't go down. Make sure the string is also under the toilet paper. In fact you should also wrap a few sheets of toilet paper around the string."

Lilly was again pleased to see how Ivan seemed to have covered everything and had made things so clear. She was more pleased when she saw the motel and how convenient it would be for her to do all her beauty stuff. They checked in as Mr. and Mrs., asked for two separate rooms and told the clerk they would return in a few hours with their drivers licenses. They handed over twelve crisp 100 bills. The clerk nodded and understood that he wasn't supposed to ask any questions. They didn't ask for a receipt. In the motel after counting out what they would need in cash Ivan showed her how to hide the money.

"I guess we're doing it differently than they did in The Godfather."

Ivan laughed. "Yeah that was one old fashioned toilet

"OK. Lil, I'll make my call now."

CHAPTER 27

"Mrs.Lyons thanks for meeting with us again. We checked with your Alanon meeting group and they indicated that anonymity would prevent them from providing any information. But when we told them we had a note from you, and we were investigating a murder, they indicated you were in attendance for the full two hour meeting. That meant you would have finished up at seven. Is that correct?"

"Yes it is Detective. I guess you still believe that I could have murdered my husband. I'm happy to fill you in with all the details. As I said I finished at seven. I stopped in a market to pick up some fish that I was going to prepare and I got home about 7: 30."

"And how did you spend the rest of the evening?"

"I cooked dinner, cleaned up and turned on the tube."

"So you never left your house once you got home."

"Well no, I took the dog out about 8 30 or so."

"Did anyone see you?"

"Yes, my neighbor. We exchanged pleasantries; her husband is in the hospital from a stroke and I asked about how he was doing and told her that I would be able to stop in tomorrow and make sure everything was OK with him. . I can give you her address and name. It's just three houses away."

"So what time did you go to bed? How much TV did you watch after you walked your dog?"

"I'm not sure. I was hoping to hear from Phil or to have him come home. I was worried so I took a hot shower and went to bed. I couldn't fall asleep right away. I don't know what time I dozed off. I know it was after midnight."

"Mrs. Lyons, Have you ever driven to Santa Monica?"

Zuma noticed that her answer did not come out as smoothly or as quickly as the others.

"I know that Phil and I have been there before. But I'm not sure I ever drove him."

"No, I meant have you ever driven it on your own?"

"If I had I would have remembered."

Zuma believed that she did remember.

"Does the name Madeline Labelle mean anything to you?"

"Other than it sounds French, it does not. I don't know anyone with that name."

"Your husband seemed to know her quite well."

"If you're telling me that she was a woman that he was involved with and implying that I know her or have met her or wanted to harm her, you are off base Detective Zuma."

"Did your husband ever mention her name to you?"

"No."

"And can you tell us the name of the perfume you use, Mrs. Lyons."

"Yes, of course it's Daim Blond from Serge Lutens."

The perfume matched the one that the search team had verified when they tested for odors in the hotel room in Santa Monica. It was unusually expensive and that was why Zuma had ruled out the "hooker" theory. The killer who had been in Phil Lyons room had expensive tastes.

CHAPTER 28

They'll meet with me tomorrow morning at ten. They weren't too happy that I missed the L.A. delivery. I didn't expect them to like it but we have made big money for them. I assume they don't want to lose that. They asked me if I had cash for them and of course I told them yes. They asked me if I was alone and I told them the truth but I didn't want the person to meet with you. Safer for both parties. They also asked if it was a man or a woman. I'm hoping they are too pissed or stupid as to dump me. But I don't have much choice. They could kill me anytime they wanted.

Karen heard the matter of fact tone in Ivan's voice. He dealt in reality. And she liked that. You needed that to survive in their world.

"We have the rest of the afternoon and evening. You do the beauty thing. I'm going to take a nap and when you get back we can go out for a nice meal.

I don't think you will have trouble getting in for your beauty stuff. They're happy to accept American cash down here and don't tip more than ten dollars. We don't want to draw any more attention to ourselves than necessary."

Lilly again thought how controlling Ivan was but it did sound like he knew what he was doing. She was excited, as she was going to do the haircut, coloring, pedicure and manicure all in one sitting. This was going to be a treat. No phone calls, no traffic. A real holiday. The hair cutting, washing, coloring manicure and pedicure took three hours and as she walked back to the motel room she began to worry. What if something happened to Ivan? What would she do? How long should she hang out? She suspected that Ivan worked pretty high up in a Mexican cartel set up. If they believed that rubbing him out would make it safer for them it would be easy to do that. He had no gun. He was alone. Bodies are part of the regular trash pick up in this town. Only if they felt he was a valuable asset or indispensible would he be OK. She also knew that no one in the drug business was indispensable. The only thing indispensable in this business was drugs.

Despite his confidence he had mentioned that he could be knocked off so she had to plan for the possibility of his not returning. She believed that she would be able to do everything they were going to do without him. Car? License? Wig? No problem for me to drive back. Even if Ivan gave her name up along with a description she would have a good fake license and Ivan's description would hardly help anyone who was looking for her. All she really had to worry about was getting out as quickly as possible, where to stay and Joe Zuma. She knew what she would do if Ivan did not return. In the interim she was going to enjoy her evening out. It had been a long time since she had gone to a bar where she didn't have to work with girlfriends and she was excited about the freedom to only worry about herself.

CHAPTER 29

When Ivan and Lilly walked into The Gaucho, for dinner the smell of whiskey and strong smoke made Lilly feel comfortable and at home. She wanted to dance immediately, resisted that temptation and began to formulate a different plan for the evening. She didn't linger debating over the many choices on the menu settling for Shrimp Tacos with extra guacamole. Ivan didn't look too knowledgeable and said

"I'll have the same, waiter. And bring us two Vodka martinis, extra olives."

They ate quickly. Ivan asked about a second drink but she said no thank you. She was in a hurry since she had a better idea of how she wanted to spend the evening. They Ubered back to the motel.

"I'll be leaving at 9 30. I'll knock on your door and coordinate some last minute things. Good night. Sleep well."

"Good night Ivan, see you in the morning"

She waited about a half hour before walking out to the beauty shop where an Uber was standing. She told the driver to take her to The Gaucho.

The place was crowded with Americans. Waitresses,mostly Latinas, looked like they had all been dressed by the same person who dressed the Vegas gals. Dark tops, lots of cleavage, very short skirts and very tall spiked heels. She thought one of them recognized her but Lilly did not nod back, She headed towards the bar for the one empty stool and before she had a chance to order she felt a tap on her right shoulder and a face leaning right over her other shoulder

"Let me buy that for you.

His face was nice but when she looked down to size him up she recognized that she must be a foot shorter than she was. She would be a fool to start dancing with this shrimp and it would make her look desperate to any of the other prospective buyers. She knew she could do much better

"No thank you. I want to buy my own and I'm looking forward to it. The short one turned away. He was not going to protest as he hardly expected this good-looking dame would let him buy her a drink.

After rejecting two more efforts at picking her up, she was glad that she had been so discriminating. The six-foot cowboy who was now leaning over her shoulder and offering to buy her a drink looked great. If he knew how to dance this could be a perfect night on the town.

"I do. I definitely do and I like to dance a lot. Let me lead you to the center of the floor. I'm sure we will both be admired. You for your looks and dancing skills; me for being the lucky one.

"OK, let's have a drink and then let's hit the floor.

It was an hour later and after two more drinks when Mr. Tall cowboy suggested they go to his room where they could continue drinking and dancing if that is what she wanted. She put her arm through his "I like your idea and it is really original."

The small guy stared at her on the way out. He was upset and angry this was going to be his lot in life. Losing out to the good-looking ones. The glare was frozen.

Cowboy noticed him and asked Lilly if she wanted him to do anything.

"He's harmless." didn't waste your energy. You'll need every drop for our evening together."

When she passed Mr. Shrimp she looked at him, smiled and blew him a kiss. The glare turned to disgust.

In the room Cowboy took out a bottle of vodka and opened a tiny plastic bag with coke. Lilly didn't hesitate and sniffed the two lines.

"Aren't you going to join me?"

"I will l need to drink a bit more. It prepares me."

"I like men who come prepared. What else are you prepared to do?"

Cowboy smiled and poured another round. After two more drinks Lilly passed out.

CHAPTER 30

Lilly was not in her room when Ivan knocked on the door at 8:30. He played through all possible scenarios. If she has been murdered, he knew he could do everything without her. He didn't want to lose her as his partner but figured that it would only be a matter of time before he would find a new one in Vegas. Maybe the Cartel folks would provide him with a connection. If she were dead he would be able to keep all the money to himself. If they found her they would torture her to find out anything about that murder and me. Nothing I need to be worried about there. If she had spent the night with someone and had overslept but was coming back he would leave her a note. All he would have to worry about was whether leaving anything in the room was OK. If she is safe and going to return before I get back she won't leave if I leave her a note. I shouldn't take the money with me because she'll think I took off and left her. When she sees the plastic in the toilet she'll know my intentions are honorable. I just have to get to the appointment.

'I left for the appointment. I should be back by noon. Be packed and ready to go.'

When Lilly woke up the cowboy was gone.

He had left her $50 but had also gone through her purse and saw that she was shy $300. It was good that Ivan had told her not to take or use credit cards. She decided not to shower and just headed back to their motel. After reading the note from Ivan she showered and packed and waited for Ivan to return .

At one o'clock she began to worry and by two she knew she had to leave. She was frantic believing they had tortured Ivan to get information about where she was. If they wanted him out of the way it was easy to see why they would also want her rubbed out. She was a witness to his last whereabouts.

She lifted the plastic bag out of the toilet, washed it off in the sink, took the cash out, stuffed it into her large purse and called an Uber. The Uber was there in less than a minute as it had just come from the beauty salon. She decided that taking the suitcase with her clothes was important. In that way if they came looking for her they would realize that by packing she was not in a rush and had a big head start. All she needed was the cash. She took it out of the plastic bag, stuffed it in in her large purse and casually stepped out of the motel. She dropped the keys right in front of the closed door and spoke to the driver as she sat down.

"Take me to a wig shop. He did not understand English but she kept pointing to her hair and he kept pointing to the beauty salon. He finally understood when she began lifting her hair up and pulling it back and pointing to her scalp hoping they would understand that she meant 'new'. Nuevo,…Nuevo,. Her getaway plan was clear in her brain.

She saw the motel owner smile as he saw the Uber pull away. He would probably show the owners $800 for the two nights and pocket the rest.

After getting a fancy wig, she would buy a used car and drive back. But to whom? And when should she call the number that Ivan had given her or should she? If this guy was Ivan's connection would the cartel know him and get to her through him? Ivan was counting on everything being OK but Lilly knew it wasn't. She remembered the piece of paper that Ivan had given her. She pulled it out and looked at the number. It seemed familiar. Oh, my god, it's the one Madeline gave me. It's Madeline's writing collaborator. Did Madeline work with two dealers? Was this guy working on a book and on some other drug deals along with her deals? Was there ever a book? Had Madeline been lying to her about the book? It was clear that she had been lying about the connection to this so-called book collaborator that Ivan was now asking her to call. Had Ivan ever mentioned her name to Mr. Maybe a book collaborator otherwise known as Mr. Definite drug dealer?

She was glad that the ride back would give her some time. Somewhere along the way before she got to Vegas or wherever the collaborator lived she would find a fancy hotel where she could do all the things that she had hoped to do on the vacation that never happened. She smiled, as she would not have to work as a gringa pushing drinks for tourists. Even with all the unanswered questions this uncharted next stage, and the drive that she would have to do alone, did not faze her. She laughed out loud realizing how much cash she was carrying. The night with the cowboy was not too expensive. She scored free drinks and coke, and the $50 seemed generous even though he had stolen $300. She relished the thought that she would not ever have to work again as a waitress. The wig was great and she was surprised and pleased that she looked so much younger. She thought that if worse came to worse and she had to go back to Vegas to work, that her new look would get her bigger tips.

CHAPTER 31

Ivan spent one minute telling three men what had happened. Two of them were in business suits and one of them was clearly the bodyguard. When asked about why he hadn't been able to deliver the money to the L.A. connection he explained that a detective had come poking around asking questions and he felt they should leave town as soon as possible.

"What did you tell him?"

"Nothing."

This information seemed to calm the two men in business suits.

"Do you know the name of the copper?"

"Yes. Joe Zuma. He's a detective out of Santa Monica."

"Why would a Santa Monica dick be poking around in Vegas?"

"He was investigating a murder. And my partner was a good friend with the gal who was murdered."

"What does that mean, 'good friend. Did the good friend know what your partner did?"

"No."

"And your partner had nothing to do with the murder right?"

"Yes. Absolutely nothing. It was a routine investigation. They look at all the people who know the vic.

"Do you think they might come back?"

Ivan knew he was on dangerous grounds. If they believed that Ivans partner would continue to be investigated, it might lead to a connection to their business.

"No". He hoped he had convinced them of something that he himself was not sure of. This information seemed to calm the two men dressed in suits who had been asking questions. Ivan knew they were getting as much information as possible so they would be prepared if Zuma was able to get closer to any of their other dealers.

"And how much cash do you have?"

"I have exactly the amount that I said earlier. I have it all here," pointing to the small pouch he was carrying. When they asked if he had come alone. He answered that he had brought his L.A. dealer with him. They casually asked where she was staying and when he told them they said that was a good choice. He smiled, and said 'she liked it because it was next to all the beauty crap that she wanted to do. They laughed, with one of them saying in English "All women are the same. Ivan heard the tall bodyguard step towards his back, felt a cold surface and heard the crack as the bullet entered the back of his head.

CHAPTER 32

"Mr. Kimball, did you bring a copy of the manuscript with you?"

"Dr. Milgram, there is no manuscript."

Jerry Paused. Had Madeline been lying all this time about her writing and her trips?

Why would she have lied? Maybe Kimball was lying.

"Can you explain that please?"

"I was in love with Madeline. I believe she loved me. The book was merely our cover for getaways to Arizona."

Gary knew that this was not going to be a therapy hour but he decided that this was his opportunity. "Look let's step outside to the Coffee Bean so that this is not a therapist client conversation and in case there is something incriminating I will not have to report it."

"I was going to ask you if you would do that. Thank you."

"So there never was a publisher and an advance? Never any writing?"

"No, not really, well, Madeline had written a few sketches about her dad and she talked to me and others and even herself about a book, but she did not work on anything while we were away."

"But Madeline was spending money. How did she get that cash?"

"I would give her a couple of grand every month."

"That's quite a bit of cash? What do you do?"

"I own apartments and have some commercial real estate as well. The money was not important. She was important. It was only a matter of time before she would leave Gary, and she would have left if he hadn't killed her."

Jerry wasn't sure of what he just heard.

"What did you say?"

"Yes he killed her. I can vouch for that."

"Well why don't you go to the police and tell them. I'm sure they would be glad to hear that you know who the killer is especially if you can prove it."

"It's proof but it's not exactly fool proof. And if it turned out that Gary would get off and knew that I was the one who accused him he would make it his business to kill me also. I'm sure he thought if he could get away with one why not two."

Jerry braced for what he knew might be a key to the case and for his chance to play a key role. He smiled inwardly as he played with the word "key" 'these two keys might make for a lock on this case.'

"O.K what is your not exact proof?"

"The night Gary came to Vegas I had been eating with Madeline in the hotel restaurant. When he came in I was in the bathroom. I hadn't ordered yet so it looked like she was alone. I decided to not go up to her and just watched from the bar and waited. I wasn't sure what she was going to do. If he would leave then I would go back and join her .But I didn't know if she might go with him. I waited and after about 20 minutes they left. I saw them getting in their separate cars and it seemed like they were heading back to L. A. I had no idea where they would be going but I was determined to know. So I followed them all the way back to a diner in Santa Monica. They were in there just for a few minutes and she came out. She was alone and began running. I started to go after her but saw Gary stepping out. He chased after her and quickly caught up to her. They walked back to the parking area and they got in their own cars. I figured she was going to be OK. I thought whatever he was angry about or accusing her of that she could talk that dumb oaf out of anything. I had a real estate deal early in the morning and had to get back to Vegas. I stepped back into the diner and fortified myself with coffee for the road. I left the diner from a side door and headed home. I'm sure they didn't see me. I was afraid of Gary. I realized when I heard the news that I had left her to be killed by her husband."

Jerry felt this guy was lying? Gary had said Madeline had hopped into a stranger's car. Was that after Kimball had left? If he was lying was it because he, Kimball, was the stranger? Her body was found in Santa Monica. Who took it there? Gary? or Kimball? or the unknown stranger?. And what about the money? If there was no advance on a manuscript, 30 grand was a lot of money for a boyfriend to give to a girlfriend. Under what grounds would he do that?

"Larry, how did you hear about Madeline's death?"

"I got the LA. Times because of my business and there was a report about a female body found next to a car in Santa Monica so I knew it was her. When I called her cell a male voice identified himself as Detective Patrick something or other so I just said, I'm sorry I dialed the wrong number.

"So what would you like me to do.? You're not exactly proof is that you saw Madeline and Gary drive off and come back. Not too good is the way I see it."

"Can you tell the police a white lie?"

"Such as?"

"A client of yours saw a male leaving a car after hearing a gunshot and the client was afraid to get involved with the police but you felt you could do this without indicating to the cops who the client was. I can provide you with a description of Gary that would steer the cops toward him. That would be my revenge on Gary for what he did to Madeline."

"I'm not sure they would buy it." Jerry was cautious with his next words. "He is probably already under suspicion.. You know how the husband is always at the top of the list."

"Oh that's right. Maybe you don't have to do anything."

"I want to be helpful and if I think of something so I don't have to lie, I will do it."

Gary thought that Kimball would know that he could go right to the police and not lie and tell them what Kimball said he saw.

"Thank you Dr. Milgram . Thank you for your time and for any help you can provide to making sure that Gary gets what he deserves. Can you please tell me how much I owe you for your time?"

Jerry hesitated; Money might make it seem to any prospective jury that he had violated confidentiality.

"No thank you. We're just two good citizens trying to help the justice system do its job."

Jerry knew that Kimball wanted him to go to the police. His description of seeing Gary coming out of the diner was not solid evidence about the murder. Why would Kimball want the police to know about him and his relationship to Madeline and her lies? Was there a manuscript and an advance? If there was, how could Kimball get away with publishing it. If there was no manuscript and that was merely a cover, why had Madeline always brought a notepad to her sessions?

"Do you have any notes that Madeline made about the book that she was or was not planning to write?"

"Yes I do and I would be happy to provide them to you. Maybe you can find something in them that I just never saw."

"Yes I would very much like to get a hold of them. How can I get them?

I'll put it in the mail tomorrow. I have your address

"Thank you, I appreciate that.

CHAPTER 33

"I know who you are. I got your number from Madeline and I also got it from Ivan.

"I don't know who you are and I don't know where Ivan is. If you want to talk with me I would have to clear it with Ivan.

"You're not going to be able to clear anything with Ivan. I'm pretty sure he will never show up. I know that he and you worked together. And I know you and Madeline worked together. And I'm not sure it was only in a manuscript."

"So why are you calling me? What do you know about Ivan? What do you mean he won't show up?"

"I think we had better meet. I believe we can do business together. I can drive anywhere to meet with you. I'm staying in Culver City."

"I'm not sure why I should meet with you. You're being too secretive. I already have a good business."

"Bully for you Mr. Dickhead. I know your business and I'm sure you want me to keep what I know to myself. I'm ready to offer you a good deal. Stop acting like a first class jerk."

"I'm in Vegas."

"Do you want to meet halfway?"

"Sure.

"How about the Apple Valley Inn, tomorrow at 11:00 a. m. I have black curly hair. I will be wearing heels, dark blue slacks and a matching blouse.

I'll be sitting in a booth and if you approach me simply say "Is your name Madeline? If you can do that I'll know it's you."

CHAPTER 34

"Hello I'd like to speak to the person in charge of the Madeline Couture case."

"Just a minute, please."

"Hi, this is Detective Zuma. How can I help you

"I saw a picture in the paper that was made of the person who was the possible murderer of Madeline Couture."

"What is your name please?"

"I'd rather not say. I own apartments in Las Vegas and a person who resembles the picture is from my neighborhood. His name is Ivan Licht."

"How would you know his name if he is only from the neighborhood."

"Everyone knows his name. We all have had several encounters and he is hardly a pleasant fellow. Frankly I'm afraid of him and that is why I want you to keep my name out of this."

Zuma signaled to Pat to put a tracer on the call.

"I will be happy to follow this up. I can ask the Vegas police to pay the gentleman a visit. Do you have his address and can you tell me anything about him?"

"He was a very quiet renter. When we argued I noticed he had an accent."

"What did you argue about?"

"He would drop his cigarettes all over the neighborhood. Other people had spoken to him but we all agreed it would be safer to say nothing."

"Anything else

"I think he lived alone and he didn't seem to spend a lot of time living there. If I were up late I would see him coming in. I think he liked to hang out on the strip. As I said he seemed to be gone every week or so for a few days."

"Thank you for this information. I hope this leads to something. By the way, did you know a Ms. Couture? I know it's a long way between Vegas and Redondo Beach but sometimes the world is a very small place."

"Yes it is a small place but I didn't know her."

"Pat get the Vegas police and have them do a stop by at the address I'm sending over to you now and have them look for a guy by the name of Ivan Licht."

"Sure boss."

Joe realized that he now had two more likely suspects; Gary the husband and this Licht character sounds suspicious. Paying in cash, trips every week or so, living alone, must be drugs.

"Boss, the Redondo police just called. Some kid found a gun on the beach near the pier. His mom turned it in. Should I tell them to run ballistics and registration?"

"Of course and tell them to rush.

"Sure boss.

"Patrick after you get hold of the Vegas police let's talk."

"No problem boss but there's a shrink out front and he says he would like to speak with you about the Couture case."

"Tell Dr. Milgram to come in, and you stay with us Pat"

"Thank you, boss."

CHAPTER 35

Kimball stood at the receptionist desk and brushed aside the request to be seated.

When he spotted the black curls and blue blouse he approached.
"Is your name Madeline?"
"Have a seat Mr. Larry Kimball."
"And to whom am I speaking?"
"I'll let you know after I say a few things and see if you're still interested. Madeline was a close friend of mine. I know the two of your worked together."

She paused. Would he think she was referring to the book or to drugs?

"At least that's what she said. I'm not sure if there is or ever was a book. She was getting more and more hyper, and manic and would have mood swings so I became suspicious but never said anything. We partied a lot but she never let anything slip about drugs. Here's my guess. A man named Ivan Licht was your connection. He got drugs for you and to you and Madeline. The two of you would move around to your clients. I don't know what the financial arrangements were nor do I care. You're up stream now without a paddle. Madeline is dead and Ivan is probably dead also.

"And how do you know that?"
"Well has he gotten in touch with you?"

Kimball nodded no. This gal knows a lot. She is probably connected to drugs also but how and with whom.

"I was in a bit of trouble and Ivan is the one who gave me your number. I didn't think you were Mr. Rogers. Ivan also worked with me and I won't tell you how; it's none of your business and it wasn't about drugs."

Kimball knew that was a lie. Ivan didn't know anyone who was not into drugs. It couldn't be romantic as this gal was too smooth and sexy for the galoot.

"O.K. all interesting so what do you want from me?"

"I want you to replace Madeline with me."

"Sorry we were lovers. Is that what you mean? You're a looker and I'm very flattered. I could certainly… Karen interrupted….

"No meathead…I can be your good little wife driving into L.A. with the stash. I keep the records and we go fifty-fifty."

Kimball became quiet. If Ivan was dead he might have trouble figuring out how to get a steady supply of drugs. He liked the idea of working with a woman.

"Sounds like a possibility how soon can you make a connection to a steady supply?"

"I can give you the name of this small town where you can go. It's in Mexico. Ask any policeman. They're all on the take and I'm sure that you can be directed to the improper authorities."

"I would prefer that we do this together. You said that you wanted to be partners."

"I'm too busy. I've got to sell my house, get rid of furniture and find a place to live."

Karen was actually afraid to be known to the cartel. She knew that she was a potential witness to Light's last whereabouts,

"Where are you thinking of living?"

"I don't know. But it won't be Vegas. I know you'd meet Madeline near Orange county so your route must have been in Southern California. It's easier on me if I lived somewhere in that area.

"What do you need me for? It cuts your profits in half. I could be an extra person for you to coordinate with. I make for more work."

"Its a cover for me. It looks less suspicious if we are driving around a lot and we're just another couple eating at different places, stopping to walk on the beach. Looks better to clients if we're a couple. And men won't hit on me.

We'd deliver the drugs, pick up cash and divvy it up and you would head back to Vegas. Your cover is your real estate business and me. I'm your girl friend. That's the way people will look at us"

"Oh is that a possibility?"

Karen looked at him seductively . "You never know what happens to people who spend a lot of time together".

She waited till she was sure he would interpret the seductive way that she intended. "Well, are you in?"

"Yes."

"OK. Here's the name of the town. There's a beauty shop next to a nice motel. You tell the motel person you're there to meet some important people and would like his help. He'll call them and they will come to you. The motel guy will let you know the time. You'll need some money. I can give you ten grand right now. How's that for trusting a partner?" She paused, "What can you give me?'

Kimball thought . He could give her something that was valuable but wouldn't be worth much unless she knew the code . He would hold on to that until he got back from Mexico.

"I have a drive, with all our clients that I'll give to you. Hold on to it till I get back.

Karen didn't think that the drive would have the exact names or addresses but she was confident that she could crack the code if Madeline or Kimball had developed it or even if Kimball didn't return.

"O.K. It's a deal. Karen also decided to add some honey."

"You seem like a fair guy."

"Thanks"

"O.K. I'll call you from Mexico as soon as I know more. I need your number." She gave him a number for one of her many throw away phones.

Kimball left cash plus a generous tip on the table. They walked out of the café together but got in their separate cars. Kimball liked the idea of more money, liked getting away from his boring real estate desk, and liked the looks on this gal. After he got into his car he realized that he didn't even know her name.

When Karen was driving back she thought, that was too easy. Maybe Madeline had been the brains and driving force. Maybe the drug money was secondary for this Kimball character and he had been in love and along for the ride. Well Mr. Kimball, I hope you enjoy the ride because that's about the only thing you will be getting out of this besides the money. She needed to find a good real estate lawyer who would help her sell the house. She hoped it would not be too difficult since Ivan had his name on the deed. She expected to hear from Kimball in three or four days and she wanted to be ready to move.

CHAPTER 36

Kimball had no trouble finding the motel When he indicated that he wanted to meet important people in town, the clerk nodded, gave him a key and spoke one word.

"Tarde."

No one showed that first night. He went back to the clerk but the word 'tarde' was repeated. The knock on the door came at seven a.m. He was still drowsy when three men barged in. One told Kimball to sit down while the other two began inspecting the place, going through the drawers, his clothing and wallet. They found the 10 grand.

"Apologies, senior we have to be careful. Now we can take you to where you want to go. Is this money for a buy?"

"Yes, it is."

"And you will be working with Mr. Licht?" The ch in the name was real Spanish.

Kimball suddenly felt strong. He had never done anything like this with Madeline. A courier had always delivered the drugs. Now he was a direct buyer dealing with higher ups from a huge cartel.

"No, I will be working alone."

"Licht was working with someone. We heard that she was a pretty senorita. Yes?

Do you know what happened to her?"

He was not sure of what to say. He liked the idea of his being the only connection. The big shot. But he also knew that he might have to count on his partner to travel down here. But he was not sure, if they had killed Licht whether they would want to get rid of her also. He thought he could always fill them in later on after some successful deals.

"I don't know about her. At this point I plan to work alone."

Suddenly the biggest one of the three was on him with a gun in his mouth.

"You had better know because if you don't we will kill you."

Kimball realized that the only power he had left was to not reveal anything. If he gave her up and they rubbed her out they would also have to get rid of him.

"All I have is a phone number. I can give that to you."

One of the men in the suits stepped out with the phone and said 'I'll be right back. After a minute when it became clear that the number was non-existent he returned.

"Thank you senior, you have been very helpful."

He nodded to the bodyguard. The bullets entered his chest, and he realized that he was going to die in the same way as his lover, Madeline Couture.

CHAPTER 37

"Gary, the ballistics on the bullet doesn't show a match on the gun you buried."

"See, I told you I didn't do it."

"But when we ran the state gun registrations we found you owned two other guns. And surprise, surprise. One of them had the same caliber."

"Where are the two guns?"

"I doubt if you're going to believe this but the truth is I sold them both at a gun show. I don't have any idea of who bought them. You can do that at gun shows. I took their money and gave them the guns."

Zuma saw smugness on Gary's face.

"Well we are going to do everything we can to find the other guns .If we do, and we find a match to the bullets that killed your wife you'll be in quite a pickle."

"It's not going to happen Lieutenant."

The smugness had turned to arrogance and pride. Gary knew that the elderly couple that bought the two guns would never use them but wanted them around to just feel safe. He doubted that they even knew how to load and fire them.

Zuma thought 'Pride before a Fall' and said goodbye .

"Boss, that guy Licht has not shown up for a few weeks. When we were asking around they said this other guy Larry Kimball had also been missing. He was the one, who collected rents."

"O.K lets get a warrant to search his place. Pat what the hell do we have left? Who do we have left?"

"We've got Silk, the husband Gary and that's it."

"Are we missing anything Pat?"

"It's hard to know what's missing when it's missing. The only thing we know we're missing is a murder weapon. We have a motive for Gary. Do we have one for Silk?

"I think we have to pay Ms. working girl another visit."

Despite the rain and thunder the trip back to Vegas was easy. He began humming the words from an old Stevie Nicks song," thunder only happens when it's raining.." to himself . He began changing the words to 'Murder only happens when ..and he filled in the words,drugs, money or sex but He couldn't get it to rhyme. Pat was quiet and he enjoyed the silence. In between his humming he went over all the conversations he had with this mess to be played over in his head.

"Boss, don't miss the turn off."

The realtor said the house had been sold. "The seller, a Ms. Karen Silk, left no forwarding address. The new owners paid cash. They were happy because the house went way below the market price. The seller was happy and the byers were very happy. This was the quickest deal I have ever done in my 20 years in the housing market. The seller said she was in a hurry and was planning to take a long vacation in South America."

"Pat let's check flights out of Vegas and L.A. to South and Central America for the last week. I'd bet she used a phony passport but maybe not. Let's put her name out to all airlines so that if she comes back under her real name we can pick her up.

"Boss, maybe she didn't even leave. Maybe she only told the realtor that, to spin a story.

"You might be right Pat. Let's figure out where she might be going instead of what she told the realtor. It's got to be away from Vegas. Now I think we have to pay a visit to the guy who likes to bury guns. Pat, do you want to go with me, back to Mr. LaBelle?"

"Sure, Boss. Do you want me to drive?

CHAPTER 38

Karen had no trouble getting a house for rent. With her new drivers license and six months rent in cash paid in advance she now needed to set up an address with the post office and get the internet going so she could look at the flash drive. After a few days of resting and eating out in different places she was restless and pushed the internet people to come out right away. Yes she was willing to pay extra.

The drive had numbers 1-126. Shit. Nothing else on it. What am I going to do? How can I crack this one? Was my ten grand for nothing? Madeline, how in hell would you come up with 126 clients? These numbers must be 126 clients. That would be one huge business. The goddamn drive must have addresses and maybe names. How would you know so many people? Where would you get a list of names? Madeline you were quiet. Your buddy from Vegas, didn't live here and he would not be able to give you that many names. Common Karen use your smarts. You always could count on them.

She had tried birth dates, initials, names of Madeline's family, Madeline's favorite drink and food;nothing worked. It took her a full three days of hacking away before she realized where she needed to look and where Madeline got the names.

"Hello, Mrs. Murray? I'm Karen and I'm sure you remember me .Yes Madeline and I were such good buds in high school. And you were the best mother. Yes I know it's a loss and I hope they find the person who did it. Yes I know the police are a pain. It's awful that they won't let you alone and just mourn. Look, I'm trying to set up a memorial for Madeline and I wanted to get hold of our high school yearbook so I can call some of our friends. You have it? That's great.

I'll only need it for a few days to call people. When can I pick it up? You're not there now but Barry is. Oh I'm sure he'll remember me. If that is O.K. with you I can be there in less than an hour. Yes I moved. I'm not living in Las Vegas any more. Tell Barry I'm on the way.

Barry was naturally suspicious of everyone but became more so when he heard that Karen had left Vegas and seemed to be less than an hour away. He also noticed that Karen looked different. If that was a face and boob job she must have lots of money. Was waitressing that good?

"So how come you left Vegas? Madeline said you had a good job at a fancy hotel."

"I got tired Barry. Wanted a change of scenery."

"Changing scenery is nice but what are you doing for a living?"

"I sold my house so I have a bit of cash and I don't need to find work immediately.

And what about you?"

"Oh, I manage."

Karen knew that was a cover. She was sure he managed but managed what?

She decided to take a chance. "Barry, I know Madeline did drugs, did she ever tell you where she got them.? I don't even have to know that. Can you help me get some light stuff, just some grass."

"I can give you some, right now."

"Thanks, that would be great. Happy to pay you."

"No… a gift to a girlfriend of Madelines. I'll tell Gary I gave it to you. It will piss him off since he is so upset about Madeline's use. Did you know she was a druggie Karen?"

"I suspected it but never asked. Thanks for the pot Barry and the yearbook. I'll get it back to your Mom in a few days. I'll make sure to invite the two of you to the memorial."

She was too excited to wait to get home so she pulled over in a gas station. Sure enough there were 126 graduates. Now could she link the names with the number? It took her about an hour to figure out that a last name's initial was first and a birthdate. The birthdate took longer as she had to track down some of the names in Google and Facebook. She was now in. She had 126 names and Madeline had indicated a yes or a no, with each address. She called the first address

"Edna? Is this Edna Allen? This is your fellow high school grad Karen Silk.

Yes, I know you're surprised .I don't know if you know this but Madeline was murdered. Oh you did know. Well I'm not just calling to let you know that . I know that Madeline visited you occasionally. There was a long pause before Edna responded.

"Yes?"

"I would like to take her place."

It took her four days to go through the list. Some of the grads just hung up. Others said they had to speak to their husbands or wives. Others wanted to meet outside their home. Others wanted to know about prices. A few said they did not have pleasant memories of Karen and asked her not to call back. In the end she had 67

67 clients who were likely candidates for sales. Now came the biggest challenge of all. How to get a reliable connection that she could rely on and whose drugs were clean? She was going to do a big, steady and reliable business in the great state of California. 'Good riddance Vegas I've don't hard time with you. No more hard times.'

CHAPTER 39

"Gary, I need to speak with you. No it's not about the gun. Nothing has shown up yet. I have a few more questions. I can be there in half an hour."

"Well we're just waiting in line at our favorite taco stand and I'm with my family."

"That will be fine with me, I'll see you soon. I'll be bringing my assistant."

The three of them, Gary, his brother and his mom, were eating tacos at a small stand.

"Gary, I want to go over the night when you last saw Madeline."

"Gee, this is just like TV."

"Shut up Barry."

"Officer why are you doing this to my son? He has proven to you that he did not kill Madeline."

"I'm sorry Mrs. Murray. I can do this at another time but Gary did say it was OK to join all of you at your lunch."

"OK, Bro tell him your alibi…No let me tell it."

"Barry, I've asked you to shut up. I'll leave with the detectives if you don't."

"Son, let Gary tell the detective what he remembers

"I told you about following her to Vegas and coming back. When I left for a moment in the diner she was gone. Some guy told me she jumped into a car and took off. I spent some time looking for her in different joints but no luck.

So what time did you leave Santa Monica and what time did you get home?

"I got home about 5.a.m.

"The coroner places the time of death around three. You could have been there when she was shot. You could have shot her."

"But I didn't."

"Detective, Gary came to my home at 4.a.m. He was very upset and told me everything."

"That still doesn't remove him from the scene of the crime.

Pat broke in, "Barry were you awakened by Gary's visit.

"No, I was sleeping."

Mrs. Murray looked surprised but tried to hide it.

Pat and Zuma caught it. They didn't know it but they both had the same exact thought. 'Another suspect has emerged. More unknowns'

"Mrs. Murray, would you be able to swear to that in a courtroom?"

"Of course detective."

The ride back in their car had two excited detectives who couldn't stop talking.

"Boss, His revenge could just be simply sibling stuff."

"Maybe, but I don't think so…He's a drug user… where does he get his stuff from?"

"Yeah, and where does he get money? Mom doesn't earn enough to support any serious habit."

"Let's put a tail on him. Follow him everywhere. Where he eats, whom he meets. Get pictures. Don't do anything with the pics. Make sure there is an address if there is a house involved.

"O.k. Boss."

CHAPTER 40

Barry had never thought much about Madeline's trips. He wasn't always aware of them as Gary never talked much. After he heard about the mileage his attention did turn to drugs. Could she be involved with that and a book? If she was and she was now dead Barry knew that someone in the drug business would be eager to fill in the gap to satisfy her clients needs.

When Karen called he thought it could be for the party honoring Madeline but when she asked for the yearbook he began thinking of her as the new dealer in town. He was surprised that she had not asked for a number for his supplier.

"Barry, I want to drop off the year book .Yes I have set up the memorial. It will be in about two months. It gives you plenty of time . Can I have the name of that person you know?" That was the request that convinced him. He would talk to her.

"So here's the deal Karen. You've got something on me. I use and I sell a little. I've got something on you. You're planning to sell, big time. I don't know where or when or even how but if I tell the police about you will become a suspect. You will not be able to move any stuff."

Karen was surprised. In high school he always seemed like the stupid younger brother.

"O.k. Let's assume your right. What else do you want?"

"I want 25% of your profits. I'll need to drive around with you to make sure what you collect."

"I could agree to that under one more condition."

"What's that?

"You get rid of those stupid tats on your neck, cut your hair and get some nice clothes. We are going to be in nice neighborhoods .You need to be presentable."

"Wow, even Mom couldn't get me to do any of that. You're quite the gal?"

Karen knew that in a few weeks she'd have him lapping at her feet.

"When do we start?"

"You'd better come up with a story for your mom. She'll be shocked at the clothes, the tats and getting out of bed early every day."

"You're right. I'll explain how Madeline's death made me feel life is short.

Karen began thinking of how she could make Barry's life much shorter.

"When do we start?"

"Call me as soon as you clean up your act and get your story straight with yours. I'll give you a place to meet. It will be a different place every morning."

"Boss, it's really strange with this Barry brother. He went into a tattoo parlor but came out with less tattoos than he went in with. He walked out of Nordstrom's with new slacks and a shirt and he cut his long hair.

"Why would our newest suspect suddenly want to look respectable? The kid has never had a real job in his life. Must be some new big deal in his life. Is there a girlfriend?"

"No boss. We've been on him 24/7."

"Keep it up. Let's see where he goes all dressed up."

CHAPTER 41

His mom told him to sit down as she took a seat right in front of him.

"Why did you lie to the detective?"

"I didn't want to become a suspect. I was out but was really worried about my life. I'm trying to turn over a new leaf Mom. I'm doing everything I can do to look respectable and get a job. No more tats, long hair, sleeping in."

"I'll believe it when I see it. But you need to tell me what you were doing when Gary came to visit me on the night Madeline was killed."

Barry felt more pressure from his Mom than from Zuma. He didn't understand it. He wondered if he should tell her. She wouldn't turn him in; She didn't give a shit about Madeline. She would become even more adamant to the police about Gary visiting her. Would she tell Gary? Would Gary turn him in? Gary was a loose screw. Lots of resentment and anger. Too much to lose. Keep your mouth shut Barry. Tell mom you were out drinking.

"Were you with anyone I know? It's hard to believe you Barry. You have a long history of lying to me. You have a long history of broken promises."

"Mom, You're right, But this whole mess with death, is this TV script playing out in our lives has bugged me. I don't want to live like a suspect in a TV drama. I want to go through life as an innocent. As a regular person."

Mom was impressed but realized she had heard those words spoken on the last crime show that her son Barry had seen. Barry came over and kissed her on the cheek. He hadn't done that in years. Maybe he was going to be a regular normal son.

"Is there something I can cook for you?"

"No Mom, I'm going out and make myself a regular. I'll pick up some food on the way home and will have a regular meal with our regular family. Call Gary and invite him. "We're a regular family

CHAPTER 42

It didn't take long for the police to record eight days of stops to clients. They had pics of Barry, a woman, and addresses. When Barry and Karen showed up at the clients for the second time they knew they could move in and arrest the two of them.

Barry and Karen knew they were in deep trouble. Drugs were in the car and the cops told her they had pictures from the last ten days. Back in their separate cells, they each pondered what they had to offer as a bargaining chip. Karen figured this was going to be a felony charge with a likelihood of 20 years. She also calculated she could help them solve the mystery disappearance of Licht and Kimball. That would be worth something in helping get a reduced sentence. She also knew that the flash drive could no longer be valuable to the cops since they probably had all her clients on tape. She wondered what Barry could say that might further hurt her. Probably nothing. The only other thing that she had that was valuable and that they might want was the information about the motel in Mexico. She had no idea if they cared about that.

The only thing that Barry had to bargain with was the knowledge of Madeline's murderer. Why would that be worth anything to them?

He knew Zuma liked to clean up his cases but if he didn't think that Barry was the killer he wouldn't care how long Barry was going to be sentenced for.

"Detective Zuma, how much is it worth to you for pleading my case as a cooperative witness in the case of a murder trial."

Zuma smiled. A guilty party to the issue being discussed usually asked that question.

"Well if it's you I couldn't tell you. If it's another person I would go to bat with you.

Barry paused, looked down, then up, took a deep breath and in a lowered voice said:

"My mother killed Madeline"

CHAPTER 43

The police raids took place in one 12 hour period. Hard drugs were found in over 100 homes and 140 people were taken into custody. Zuma and Pat and the Orange County Police were on TV for two nights in a row when Zuma decided that enough was enough. He told Pat he could have his 15 minutes of fame every night from now till interest in the drug busts waned. He could now focus on Barry and Mrs. Murray.

"Thanks, Boss.will I have to get a suit or can I wear the uniform".

"Ask the people wanting to interview what they want. You can also tell them where you think they would get the most interesting shots. You can use the station as background or any of the other sites where crimes occurred. When you answer all these requests on my desk, be friendly to them. It's good PR for us and they will be helpful in the future. But first, pick Mrs. Murray up for the murder of her son.

"Sure boss, I can do it alone or should I follow protocol.

"Pat you know what my answer to that question is going to be. Get going."

CHAPTER 44

"Barry, what the fuck is going on. Mom's been arrested and charged. Did you have anything to do with this?"

"No. I don't know what evidence they have. I'm as surprised as you are."

"Well how the hell could she have done it? She was home when I got there and the murder had occurred. Mom doesn't drive fast at night. She can hardly see."

"Gary, you can tell your story. Let's hope they believe you. I'm a criminal who's going to jail for drug dealing. At least I'll look good in the courtroom. I'll look like a successful businessman"

"Shit, you're worried about how you'll look while mom is facing a death sentence. You are a sicko."

"I'll be out in a few years. First offense. Good, expensive lawyer."

"Yeah that you're paying with all your drug dealing."

And Gary, dear brother, where did you think all the money went from your years of grass using. Let me tell you older brother. It went to pay for good lawyers. It's America. We deal drugs. Cops get hired. Judges get hired. Vics need social workers. Our taxes pay the social worker. Dealers pay lawyers. Convicts need prisons. States pay for construction. Our taxes go to the states. It's all connected. We're all connected.

"And you got that from TV?"

"Some of it from T.V. Most of it I learned doing big business in our wonderful Orange County. I was a successful businessman. You weren't. Madeline was right."

"Maybe. But if you're so damn successful how come you're going to jail. Smart businessmen don't make dumb choices. If it came down to choices my life is better than yours is going to be."

"I'll be joining a long list of successful business people who go to jail. In this country you can do business in one of two ways. You can be honest and be poor or you can be crooked and be rich."

"I don't think you're right. I think you're just blowin smoke. There's got to be an honest business that's also successful."

"Successful, yes, but not big. I was big."

CHAPTER 45

Zuma looked at Gary who seemed more distraught than he had ever seen.

"She couldn't do such a thing Detective. She wouldn't do such a thing. She can hardly see at night. She never goes out at night. When I got there she was sleeping. You gotta believe me."

"I want to find the person who murdered your wife Gary, but we have testimony from what seems like a reliable witness. And we have a motive. Your Mom detested Madeline. The only thing that might prove her innocence is the murder weapon.

Did anyone have access to your home that would allow him or her to get your gun? Do you know anyone who would know where you kept it?

"My mom has a key and she can get in at any time."

"Where does she keep the key?"

"It's not hidden if that's what you mean. It just hangs on the back of the front door."

"So anyone who knew what the key was for could have taken it."

"Yes."

"That leaves your Mom and your brother."

Look Detective Zuma, I know no one believes I'm smart, but I will figure this out. It couldn't be my mom. Zuma agreed privately but said nothing. He welcomed the added nose in the case.

"Gary I think you're too close to this. You're agitated and upset. I think you might benefit from seeing Madeline's therapist. He might be able to help you sort through this mess."

"Thanks, Detective. I like that idea."

Zuma had been receiving lots of kudos on the Orange county busts. The precinct looked good. Interviews were being conducted and Zuma made sure that many of his fellow detectives received attention. His captain was suggesting a promotion and an extra week of vacation. A network exec had contacted him about a TV series based on the breaking of this middle class bust.

He passed all of the interviews he could to Pat. There was a lot of noise already and there would be more. The idea of a vacation was appealing but he didn't want to leave town with any loose ends. And the killer with only one person's testimony and a motive was still a loose end.

CHAPTER 46

Dr. Mailgram spoke softly. "We are going to work differently today."

"I really need your help Dr, Milgram."

"I know and I'm going to help you Gary. You'll need a pad and a pencil, I have one here. We're going to do this slowly. We are not in a rush. You will be doing what you know how to do."

Gary takes the pad and pencil and draws a picture of a woman jumping into a car

"Put a time on it." 1:30 am."

"Now write the time underneath the picture when Malila was shot. 2: am"

"Now put the time you arrived at moms. 3: am"

"If mom had done it she couldn't be back home and in her nightgown by three."

He stares and stares at the numbers, the figures and the imagined drive. It was like his tile work. How could he put the pieces together so they would all lock?

There had to be a key to this puzzle. The key. The key. That's what made him realize that Barry could have done it.

"Talk out loud about what you are thinking.

"I'm thinking of how Barry could have done it. Madeline jumps in the car with Barry. Of course she doesn't like him but is trying to get away. It's one thirty and they have an argument. Maybe it was about drugs. He calms her down and invites her to get in the back seat so they won't be noticed. She gets in. He grabs her neck, pushes it down, shoots her and dumps her body outside the diner and drives home. He could have returned the gun any time the next day when he saw me leave. I find the gun and panic. Wonder if there are any bloodstains in the car?

"Why don't you call Zuma and tell him to pick up Barry's car and look for stains and a possible match with Madeline's.

"Son of a bitch. I'll kill him.

"That's not a good idea Gary. Let's plan this out. You are planning to confront him. He will probably deny it. If he admits to it I want you to just turn around and leave. Can you do that?

"I think so."

"No 'I think so'. I need your word. What are you going to do if he denies it?"

"I'll tell him the police are searching his car for blood stains."

"NO. No. That puts you in jeopardy. I want you to say 'I guess the jury will decide.'

"Can you also agree to that?"

"Yes."

"Good.Im going to go with you to your home in Redondo. I'll wait outside the door. When you go in make sure it's not locked so I or the police can get in quickly if there is trouble."

The drive back was without a word. Jerry was happy that he was finally getting involved. Hopefully this would help prevent another murder and solve another.

"Hey Barry baby, I know you did it. You took the key to the house, stole my gun, used it to kill her, drove back and returned the gun the next day."

"A fancy tale Bro. You must have started to watch those TV dramas also.

"Will see if it's a phony tale. Well see if those are phony blood stains in your car.

"You big assed,big boned brother. I did kill her and it was easy. Mom didn't like her, she treated me like shit . And I'm getting back at you

"For what?

"For all the baseball games you wouldn't invite me to play with you .For the surfing you did and made fun of me and wouldn't teach me. For all the years that you were moms' favorite. I'm getting back, and with that he lunged and swung an upper fist aimed at Gary's jaw. It was an easy dodge.

By the time the police got there and broke down the door that Gary had locked.

Both brothers were lying on the floor bleeding. Knives and mom's big frying pan had been used.

CHAPTER 47

In the hospital Gary told Zuma that Barry had admitted the murder but he was not going to rely on his word against mine so he tried to kill me. "I guess he forgot he was always the little brother."

"The bloodstains checked out Gary. They were Madeline's. You did a good job. I don't think Mom is going to be too upset when she finds out that her own son was willing to send her to prison. She might be extra proud of you for figuring the whole thing out."

"What did Barry say when you visited him, Detective?"

"He didn't want to speak to me. He says he's been advised to say nothing by his lawyer."

Zuma made the phone call upon leaving the hospital.

"Hi Dr. Milgram, thanks for helping Gary figure it out and more thanks for calling the cops when you heard the scuffling. You were a big help and I'll remember it. I hope I can call upon you again.

"I usually say I can hardly wait but I think seeing the two of them on the floor with all that blood made me wary. I think I need a vacation.

"Funny you should say that. I need one also."

CHAPTER 48

Gary was able to get some of the money that Madeline had stashed away from Kimball. He bought a new truck, and hired his mom as a foreman. On the truck he painted "'A MOM and SON TILE BUSINESS '. Underneath in smaller lettering

'Were local and we bring brightness and color into your daily life.'

Mom showed up every day with her old frying pan and banged it to let the workers know it was time for their 15 minute break. She banged it again and if they didn't get back in time and she had no trouble firing them. She had a supply of fish tacos that she kept warm, and guacamole that she kept cold for her workers and for potential clients. The workers had never been given free food on their breaks and after a while neither Gary nor she had to worry about finding new employees. She was good at greeting visitors who dropped in casually to see the work and the business slowly picked up. Gary was now employing four people and could pay attention to how the employees performed. He became less afraid of firing them if they weren't performing. If they didn't call in or if they were consistently late he knew that Moms pan would not wear out. She liked working with her son and enjoyed telling people how she made the tacos and the guacamole. Gary began thinking about expanding the business. He wished that Madeline could see that he was being successful.

Zuma was delighted to hear from Pat how good the tacos and guacamole tasted and how successful the business was. He was glad that another local food option rather than another chain option had been created.

It was too far for him to travel and support daily. He would just have to feel good about the small, personal garage that he now used. He was also planning upon taking his boys to eat at Garys when his boys came to visit.

CHAPTER 49

He was back in the cape in Truro and getting his first load of groceries at Jams. He was lucky to get the same house as he had last year. He noticed her as she was waiting in line for a muffin. He never had forgotten her body contours. He tapped her on the shoulder

"I think I owe you a drink but would you settle for a muffin?"

"That's a good offer for the morning. But I hope it's only the first one. I know you can do better. I have been waiting for you."

"So have I. It's been a long wait but it now seems worth it.

They sat in silence outside the café. He was filled with cheer enjoying their silence knowing they would have lots of time to talk about lots of things.

"I don't want to rush things but I have to get back to unload these groceries. I'd love to take you to dinner this evening or I'd be happy to make it.

"I knew I could count on you for the better offer. Home cooking sounds best

After dinner when they were sitting on the porch looking at the stars in the clear sky. Their fingers were interlocked. Zuma thought about the gigantic space in the heavens that always brought him peace. There was only a tiny space that separated him now from the woman whom he had just fed. It gave him a deeper sense of peace than the heavens could.

He was going to have one week with Claudia before his boys showed up. He knew they would be happy to meet her. It would make it clear to them that he had not only come back but gone forward. There was no tin can to kick down the street. There was no sign that showed him the way. He didn't need a sign. And it didn't matter that it was gonna rain tomorrow or every day from now on.

THE END

www.ingramcontent.com/pod-product-compliance
Lightning Source LLC
Chambersburg PA
CBHW030336100526
44592CB00010B/713